Can't wait to see what's next!
Frances C., Carleton Place ON

Your recipes are a great success.
Mary S., Brockville ON

Looking forward to new shows and a new cookbook!
Patricia S., Pierrefonds QC

I am really enjoying PamCooks. *It's a real gem for my cookbook collection.*
Jean A., Otter Lake QC

Just a few of the hundreds of letters Pam received in response to *PamCooks* and her appearances on *News at Noon*. As a result, we're pleased to offer another helping of Pam Collacott with:

PamCooks 2

• • •

Pint-sized chefs join us on the CJOH set at Trillium Cooking School

Front row: Nathalie Ruttle, Alexander Kealey, Monika Ruttle
Back row: Pam Collacott, Karen Lewis, Korin Kealey, Celia Armitage, Leanne Cusack

Every two weeks, for the past six years, I've been lucky enough to be one of Pam Collacott's official taste-testers. We get to cook on live TV and eat the creations. What a great gig! I'm lucky to experience Pam's casual culinary genius first-hand.

Pam's recipes have become so famous that she can boast, although she never would, thousands of hits on her website after each show. Where I see their popularity...going through the register at the grocery store when the cashier asks about about Tabouleh with a Twist *(page 79)*, or going through security at the airport when a security person comments on the Ginger Lime Salmon in Parchment *(page 60)*. Viewers enjoy Pam's warmth and her comfortable approach to making what have been perceived as tricky or challenging dishes. She makes delicious recipes for people with busy lives.

I can personally attest to the scrumptious qualities of the recipes and meal plans that follow. No potluck would be complete without Mexican Lasagna *(page 55)*, a holiday gathering will be more memorable with the Cider-Glazed Pork Tenderloin with Carmelized Onion and Apple Stuffing *(page 44)*, and the Ginger Pear Upside-Down Cake *(page 108)*...well, it's a must. Bake two: one for dessert, one for breakfast.

— Leanne Cusack

BREAKFAST FOR LEARNING
Canadian Living Foundation

The Breakfast for Learning Canadian Living Foundation

A message from founding board member Elizabeth Baird,
food and nutrition editor of *Canadian Living* magazine

When Pam Collacott first heard about Breakfast for Learning, she knew this was a foundation she wanted to support. Started in 1992 by editors of *Canadian Living* magazine, Breakfast for Learning has helped over 6,900 community nutrition programs from coast to coast to coast, and is unwavering in the commitment of ensuring that every child in Canada goes to school well nourished and ready to learn.

Pam's experience with enabling children to take up the challenge of a day at school goes back to the '70s, to her own experience teaching home economics in an Ottawa inner-city school. For the needy children in her school, she set up a breakfast program, providing steaming bowls of porridge, hot chocolate, fresh oranges, a little mothering and more—all with positive results. When Pam and husband Read had their own children, Amy and Brian, Pam moved her teaching career to her own cooking school and invited children into the world of food, empowering them to gain cooking skills. It saddened Pam to see home economics dropped from so many schools, leaving children no place to acquire cooking basics, and just as important, healthy eating savvy.

For Pam, Breakfast for Learning addresses the immediate problem of hungry children, as it also educates them about the importance of a nutritious diet. Back in 1999, when she published *PamCooks*, a delicious volume, now in its second printing and based on her lively and charming cooking segments with host Leanne Cusack on CJOH-TV News at Noon, Pam decided to donate part of the proceeds to the Breakfast for Learning Foundation. Now with this new cookbook *PamCooks 2*, Pam has reaffirmed her desire to help kids get a fair shake in the classroom by again offering a percentage of her proceeds to Breakfast For Learning.

Pam Collacott is one of 30,000 volunteers who take time out of their day and money out of the wallets to help Canadian children. As a founding board member of Breakfast for Learning, I am proud that the foundation has Pam Collacott's support. Please join Pam and Breakfast for Learning. For more information on how you can help, please visit the foundation's website at www.breakfastforlearning.ca.

PamCooks

More
Favourites
from the
Trillium
Cooking
School

2

by Pam Collacott

Foreword by Anne Lindsay

Published by Creative Bound Inc.
on behalf of
Trillium Cooking School
R.R.#2
North Gower, ON K0A 2T0

ISBN 0-921165-77-3
Printed and bound in Canada

Production by Baird, O'Keefe Publishing Inc.
Publication Specialists
Gail Baird, Managing Editor
Wendy O'Keefe, Creative Director

Editing by Korin Kealey
Graphics, cover design by Brian Collacott
Author photo, front cover, by Lynn Ball
Photo, back cover, by Valberg Imaging

National Library of Canada Cataloguing in Publication

Collacott, Pam, [date]
    PamCooks 2 : more favourites from the Trillium Cooking School /
Pam Collacott

Includes index.
Co-published by Trillium Cooking School
ISBN 0-921165-77-3

1. Cookery. I. Trillium Cooking School II. Title. III. Title: PamCooks 2.

TX714.C592 2002   641.5   C2002-902974-0

Acknowledgements

It's been two years since we published *PamCooks* and I must say I've been surprised and delighted by the response to it. So many complimentary words, so much enthusiasm to try the recipes, so much fun visiting communities in the Ottawa area and beyond to cook for and meet so many wonderful people.

Surprisingly, it was my husband Read who convinced me to get to work on *PamCooks 2*. And I'm glad he did. Once again it was difficult to decide which of the hundreds of recipes to include and which ones had to be reluctantly left out. The letters and comments of viewers who watch Leanne and I cook on CJOH-TV helped in the decision too, and I thank all of you for that. I also thank the following family members and friends for their help and support:

Read Collacott—My husband of 33 joyous years, my best friend and most enthusiastic and helpful recipe test guinea pig! You are always nearby with a warm smile, a timely joke, a helping hand, and a welcome hug. I am truly blessed.

Leanne Cusack—Viewers still comment, "You two look like you're having so much fun" when they watch us cook together. After 7 years of culinary conspiracy and cooperation, we often anticipate each other's questions and end each other's sentences! You still inspire me with your professionalism, warm and generous personality and fabulous sense of humour. I have learned so much from you and look forward to many more years of friendship and kitchen camaraderie.

Amy Collacott—You have literally grown up beside my stove and it's delightful to me that some of my food enthusiasm has rubbed off on you. You have been a wonderful help with my work and the cakes that you make and decorate are beautiful, artistic and delicious. Thanks so much for your enthusiastic help and creative input. Looking forward to lots more shared kitchen time even after you and Jeff are married!

Brian Collacott—Since Brian created the graphics for *PamCooks* two years ago, he has gone back to school to intensively study graphic design. The results of his studies are seen in the attractive cover and beautiful graphics he created for this book. We're very proud of your accomplishments, Brian, and I'm very grateful for your work on this project.

Dorothy Searles—My mom, who inspired me to focus more attention on the value of cooking good food for yourself, even if you live alone, and who provided several more of her delicious recipes for this book. Thanks, Mom!

Elizabeth Baird—Even though my mom now challenges how I cook with "Elizabeth doesn't do it that way!" I still regard you as Canada's best gift to good cooking. It's wonderful being your friend and sharing food experiences and adventures with you, on and off the ski trails! Breakfast for Learning is fortunate to have you as their spokesperson.

Anne Lindsay—Ever since we met in the early '80s, you have been enthusiastic and generous with friendship, support and help to me and many others who follow your example of dedication to healthy eating and good food. Thank you from a friend and a fan of your excellent work. I'm lucky to have you as my mentor.

"Rellies" and Friends—You enthusiastically promoted *PamCooks*—here we go again! Special thanks to my sisters Deb, Karen, Cathy and Mary Pat and their spouses, in-laws Enid and Brian, Susan and Tony, nieces, nephews, the "golf girls"(Cheryl, Jo-Ann, Joan and Wendy), Martha and Warren and all my friends, the students and teachers who come to the Trillium Cooking School. Such wonderful friends and avid booksellers! Warm thanks to all of you, and keep up the good work!!

Karen Lewis—You become more indispensable as time goes on! Leanne and I flounder when you aren't there to keep us on time, tidy and smiling at your humorous observations. Thanks so very much from two grateful fans!

Korin Kealey—Thank you for the excellent job you did editing this book, and for being such a creative and enthusiastic food friend.

My Friends at CJOH—Thanks to Garry Bitze, Caroline Ives, Michael O'Byrne (glad you finally made it out to cook with us this year!), cameramen Larry, Serge, Randy, Paul, Dan, Harvey, Brian and John, Chris and Donnie "out in the truck," Maria who prints the recipe sheets, and everyone at CJOH—you make us look so good on the air and make me feel so welcome when I come to the station. My heartiest thanks to all of you!

Lynn Ball—Photographer and friend. Thank you for braving the blackflies to shoot the cover of this book one sunny but buggy May afternoon!

Gail, Wendy, Louise, Jill, Lindsay and Maureen at Baird O'Keefe Publishing Inc. and Creative Bound Inc.—It's been 10 years since we first worked together. Now we've completed our third joint project, and once again I'm grateful and appreciative of your help and willingness to work to almost impossibly short deadlines. Heartfelt thanks!

Food Friends—Members of Cuisine Canada and the International Association of Culinary Professionals—so many food friends, only an e-mail or phone call away with help, inspiration and support. Thanks to all of you!

To the CJOH *News at Noon* Viewers—This book wouldn't have happened if you hadn't asked for it, and I thank you for your many letters, e-mails, cards and kind and complimentary words and suggestions.

My wish is that you take time to prepare the recipes in this book, and to lovingly share them with family and friends. The camaraderie of the table is as much a part of a healthy diet and happy life as the food itself.

Pam Collacott

Contents

Foreword by Anne Lindsay 9

Appetizers 11

Brunch 25

Kids Cook 31

Main Dishes
    Beef 38
    Lamb 43
    Pork 44
    Poultry 47
    Seafood 56
    Vegetarian 64

Salads 72

Side Dishes
    Rice 80
    Vegetables 82

Soups 91

Sweets
    Candy 99
    Cookies 100
    Squares 102
    Cakes 105
    Pies 114
    More Treats! 121

The Last Word—More Help for Busy Cooks 128

Index 129

Foreword

by Anne Lindsay
Author of best-selling cookbooks, including *Smart Cooking* and *Lighthearted Everyday Cooking*

I first met Pam in 1984 when the International Association of Culinary Professionals (IACP) held their annual conference in Toronto. Sixteen food writers and cooking school teachers entertained the delegates in their homes for dinner. Carol Ferguson and I hosted a dinner in my home in Toronto, and Pam Collacott, who lives in Ottawa and was also attending the conference, volunteered to help us.

Pam met me for the first time, walked into my kitchen, donned her apron, rolled up her sleeves, and for the next 5 to 6 hours, chopped ingredients, passed hors d'oeuvres, removed the Navarin of Lamb from the oven at just the right time, and never stopped until every plate was clean and put away. She is the type of person who can walk into anyone's kitchen and just knows what to do and how to help. Pam and I have been friends ever since. Pam has continued to be very involved with IACP, and for a number of years worked hard as a volunteer, raising money for their scholarship programs.

At the time we first met, neither of us had written a cookbook or cooked on television. Since then, Pam has written four cookbooks and been a regular guest on Ottawa's CJOH-CTV *News at Noon*. She has hosted a television program on cooking with children, and for many years wrote a food column for the *Ottawa Citizen*. She has been a regular contributor to numerous magazines, including *Canadian Living*, and throughout all of this, she has run her successful Trillium Cooking School, where I have had the happy experience of being a guest teacher.

One of the reasons that I always look forward to promoting my cookbooks in Ottawa is that Pam does the food styling for my television appearances. Cooking for live television can be a little nerve-racking; however, Pam makes it easy because she always has everything perfectly organized and prepared, and she makes beautiful food.

Speaking of beautiful food, Pam's recipes not only look good, they taste great. *PamCooks 2* has an appealing selection of recipes from traditional favorites, such as Guacamole, Coquilles St Jacques and Coq Au Vin, to new dishes, such as Mexican Lasagna and Seafood Grilled on a Cedar Plank. There are recipes for children and for cooking for one person. The recipes are well tested and easy to follow. I know you will enjoy cooking from this new book—this is tasty food, prepared with Pam's love of good cooking.

Crab Melts

Makes 24 pieces

You probably have in your pantry most of what you need to make these delicious little bites. You'll love how fast and easy they make up. Your guests will love how terrific they taste.

    1 6-ounce (170 g) tin crabmeat, drained, flaked
    1/2 cup light mayonnaise
    1/3 cup grated Parmesan cheese
    1/4 cup chopped green onion
    2 tablespoons minced red pepper
    1 tablespoon chopped fresh dill or parsley *(optional)*
    1 tablespoon fresh lemon juice, or to taste
    1 baguette, cut into slices 1/2-inch thick

1. In medium bowl, stir together all ingredients except bread. Spread mixture on baguette slices.

2. Place slices on baking sheet. Broil until topping is brown and bubbly. Serve hot.

Make Ahead

Cooled puffs can be frozen in a tightly covered container for up to 2 months.

Reheat on baking sheet at 350°F for about 8 minutes.

Cheddar Puffs

Makes about 4 dozen

Perfect with a bowl of soup for lunch, or with a glass of wine at a party.

> 1 cup water
> 1/2 cup butter
> 1/4 teaspoon salt
> 1 cup all-purpose flour
> 3 to 4 eggs
> 3/4 cup shredded sharp cheddar cheese, divided
> 1 to 2 tablespoons sesame seeds

1. Measure water, butter and salt into medium saucepan; bring to boil.

2. Remove from heat; add flour all at once. Return to burner; set to medium. Stir constantly until mixture is smooth and pulls away from sides of pan. Remove from heat.

3. Add eggs one at a time, beating well after each addition and adding only enough of the last egg to make a mixture that still holds its shape when dropped from a spoon. Beat in 1/2 cup of the cheese.

4. Drop spoonfuls or pipe smalls mounds of batter onto a greased or parchment-lined baking sheet. Leave at least 1 inch between mounds. Sprinkle with sesame seeds and remaining cheese. Bake in preheated 375°F oven for 25 to 35 minutes, or until puffed and golden. For crisper puffs, pierce top of each puff with a sharp knife and bake 5 minutes more. Serve warm.

Great Guacamole

Makes about 1 1/2 cups

You'll have a hard time finding a guacamole that tastes better than this one. Thanks to my lifelong friend, Patti Miller, for sharing this recipe with me when we visited her in Phoenix, Arizona, many years ago.

    1 clove garlic
    2 large, ripe avocadoes
    2 tablespoons lime juice
    1/3 cup finely chopped onion
    1/2 teaspoon salt, or to taste
    1/2 of a 4.5-ounce (127 mL) tin chopped green chilies
    1/3 cup finely diced tomato

1. Purée garlic, avocado and lime juice in food processor or mince garlic and mash avocado mixture by hand. Stir in remaining ingredients. Taste and adjust seasonings. Cover and chill until needed.

2. Serve with tortilla chips or as a topping for tacos, fajitas or other Mexican favourites.

Minted Melon Limeade

Add crushed mint leaves to tall glasses of limeade or lemonade. Add ginger ale or club soda for sparkling version.

Garnish each serving with mint sprigs, lemon or lime slices and fresh strawberries.

Cleaning Mushrooms

Because mushrooms absorb water easily and become soggy, avoid soaking them during cleaning.
If they are very dirty, run them quickly under cold water and immediately pat dry with paper towels.

For most mushrooms, use a damp paper towel or mushroom brush to remove any dirt, and trim the end of the stem if necessary.

Italian Stuffed Mushrooms

Makes 2 dozen pieces

My friend Cheryl Fleming introduced me to these decades ago, and they have been a family favourite ever since.

24 medium mushrooms, cleaned
2 slices bacon, finely chopped
2 green onions, minced
1 small clove garlic, minced
1/4 teaspoon dried oregano
1/2 cup shredded mozzarella
1/4 cup dry breadcrumbs
1 tablespoon minced fresh parsley
Salt and freshly ground pepper to taste

1. Clean mushrooms; remove stems by twisting then separating from caps. Chop stems finely. Place caps on baking sheet.

2. In medium skillet, sauté bacon until almost cooked. Stir in chopped stems, green onions, garlic and oregano; cook and stir until onions are soft and bacon is crisp.

3. In medium bowl, stir together bacon mixture, cheese, breadcrumbs and parsley. Season to taste with salt and freshly ground pepper. Fill caps with bacon mixture. (Can be prepared to this point several hours ahead. Cover tray with plastic wrap and refrigerate until serving time.)

4. Broil caps until filling bubbles and browns. Serve hot.

"Lighter than Hummus" Chickpea Spread

Makes about 1 1/2 cups

Great for dipping or as a spread on sandwiches, pita bread or tortilla wraps.

2 cloves garlic
1 19-ounce (540 mL) tin chickpeas, drained, rinsed
Juice of 1 lemon
2 tablespoons minced parsley or cilantro
2 tablespoons light sour cream
1 green onion, chopped
Salt and freshly ground pepper
Baked Sesame Tortilla Wedges *(see sidebar)*

1. With food processor running, drop garlic through feed tube; process until finely chopped. Add chickpeas, lemon juice, parsley or cilantro, sour cream, onion, and a sprinkling of salt and pepper; process until smooth. Taste and add more lemon juice, onion, parsley, salt or pepper, as needed.

2. Store in refrigerator. Serve with baked tortilla wedges, warm pita bread or raw vegetables. Can be made a day ahead.

Baked Sesame Tortilla Wedges

Makes 48 pieces

6 small flour tortillas
1 egg white, beaten
1/4 cup sesame seeds

Brush one side of each tortilla with egg white. Sprinkle with sesame seeds. Use pizza cutter or scissors to cut each tortilla into 8 wedges. Place on baking sheet.

Bake in preheated 375°F oven for 8 to 10 minutes, or until lightly browned. Serve with your favourite low-fat dip.

Picnic Time

Freeze Make-Ahead
Antipasto in 1- or 2-
cup containers,
ready to defrost as
needed. Pack a still-
frozen container in
your cooler when you
head to the beach or
boat. It will defrost
by lunchtime and
help to keep the
rest of the picnic
food cool all morning.

Make-Ahead Antipasto

Makes 10 to 12 cups

I've been making this antipasto for years and never get tired of its tangy flavour. It takes a while to get all the vegetables chopped and measured, but you'll be glad you took the time whenever you take a carton of it out of your freezer to serve to family and friends. Omit the tuna for a vegetarian version.

    4 carrots, peeled and thinly sliced
    1 green pepper, seeded, chopped
    1 sweet red pepper, seeded, chopped
    1 cup chopped celery
    1 cup tiny cauliflowerets
    1 12 1/2-ounce (375 mL) tin sliced black olives, drained
    1 cup sliced mushrooms, fresh or canned
    1 cup small white pickled onions
    2 cups chopped sweet pickles
    1 cup chopped stuffed olives (use salad olives; they're already chopped)
    1 14-ounce (398 mL) tin tomato sauce
    1 1/3 cups ketchup
    3 tablespoons olive oil
    2 6-ounce (170 mL) tins water-packed solid tuna, drained, flaked

1. Place all ingredients except tuna in large saucepan. Stir to mix; cover and cook over medium heat until boiling. Stir occasionally.

2. Turn heat to low; cover pot and cook until carrots are tender-crisp. Stir occasionally.

3. Add tuna to the cooked vegetable mixture. Transfer to serving-size containers and refrigerate for 2 weeks, or freeze for up to 3 months.

4. Serve with crackers.

Maple Chicken Wings

Makes 30 pieces

Similar to my Mom's fabulous baked wings, but with an added touch of maple syrup. The longer they cook, the better they taste.

15 chicken wings
1 cup dark brown sugar
1/3 cup each, maple syrup and dark soy sauce
1 large clove garlic, minced
1 tablespoon cornstarch

1. Cut each wing into 3 pieces at joints. Discard wing tips. Trim excess fat from remaining pieces. Arrange wing pieces in a single layer in lightly greased or sprayed baking pan large enough to hold them in a single layer.

2. In small bowl, mix brown sugar, maple syrup, soy sauce, garlic and cornstarch until cornstarch dissolves; pour over chicken. Stir until wings are coated with the mixture.

3. Cover pan with foil. Bake at 375°F for 30 to 45 minutes. Remove foil; continue baking for 30 to 40 minutes more, or until wings are very tender and sauce is slightly thickened. Baste with sauce and rotate wings occasionally during cooking. Can be made a day ahead and reheated.

Marinated Mushrooms

Makes about 4 cups

These tangy morsels disappear quickly whenever I serve them. Take them to your next potluck and see for yourself. They make an excellent hostess gift at holiday time, but must be kept in the refrigerator.

> 1/2 cup red or white wine vinegar
> 1/3 cup olive oil
> 2 cloves garlic, crushed
> 1 small dried hot chili, crushed
> Few whole peppercorns
> 2 tablespoons water
> 1 teaspoon sugar
> 1/2 teaspoon each, salt, dried basil, rosemary and thyme
> 1 pound small mushrooms, cleaned

1. In saucepan on stovetop or in large glass measure in microwave, bring all ingredients except mushrooms to a boil. Stir in mushrooms; cook 3 minutes more.

2. Place in covered glass container; refrigerate overnight or up to 1 week. Stir occasionally.

3. Sprinkle with minced parsley when serving. If giving as a gift, tell recipient to store in refrigerator and use within 1 week.

Roasted Red Pepper Hummus
Makes about 2 cups

The rosy colour and sensational flavour of this savoury spread makes this hummus extra special.

    2 large red bell peppers, roasted, peeled, chopped
    1 19-ounce (540 mL) tin chickpeas, drained, rinsed
    1/4 cup olive oil
    1 tablespoon sesame oil, or more to taste
    Juice of 1 large lemon, or to taste
    1/4 teaspoon ground cumin
    1 large clove garlic, crushed, or more to taste
    2 tablespoons minced fresh parsley or cilantro
    Salt and pepper to taste
    Warm pita bread wedges

1. To roast peppers, place on grill or under broiler until skin on all sides blackens and blisters. Rotate pepper as needed. Place blackened peppers in paper bag or under a tea towel until cool enough to handle. Peel off and discard blackened skin. Remove and discard stem and seeds. Chop pulp.

2. In food processor, purée peppers, chickpeas, olive oil, sesame oil, lemon juice, cumin and garlic until mixture is smooth. Stir in cilantro or parsley. Season to taste, adding salt and pepper as needed.

3. Spoon into serving dish. Garnish with cilantro or parsley sprigs. Serve with warm pita bread wedges, or use as a sandwich spread.

Freezing Roasted Red Peppers

When red peppers are in season in the summer and early fall, grill and freeze them in quantity to enjoy in the winter when the price of fresh peppers is exorbitant. The texture and flavour of defrosted roasted red peppers is very similar to fresh roasted. After grilling, layer between sheets of waxed paper, place in freezer bags, label and freeze until needed. Defrost on paper towels to absorb excess moisture.

Seafood Appetizer Platter

Serves 8 to 10

At holiday time, prepare this colourful appetizer on a Christmas tree-shaped platter, as my friend Caroline Ives suggests.

1 8-ounce (250 mL) package light cream cheese, softened
1/4 cup light sour cream
1/4 cup ketchup
2 to 3 teaspoons horseradish
4 ounces small cooked shrimp
4 ounces crabmeat
Minced fresh dill, parsley and green onion
Slivered red pepper to garnish
Crackers

1. Combine cream cheese and sour cream until smooth. Spread in a layer on a 12-inch diameter platter.

2. Mix ketchup and horseradish to taste; spread over cheese layer.

3. Arrange shrimp, crab, dill, parsley and green onion in an attractive pattern on top of horseradish mixture. Serve with crackers.

Sun-Dried Tomato Tapenade

Makes about 3/4 cup

The intense flavour of this savoury spread will transport you to the sunny Mediterranean. It's the perfect starter for your next barbecue.

1/2 cup sun-dried tomatoes (not oil-packed)
1 clove garlic
1 tablespoon chopped fresh basil
1 tablespoon chopped parsley
1 teaspoon capers
2 anchovies, chopped
Dash Worcestershire and Tabasco sauces, to taste
1 teaspoon extra virgin olive oil
Pepper to taste

1. Place tomatoes in small bowl; pour enough boiling water over to cover. Let stand 1/2 hour. Drain well; reserve liquid.

2. Place tomatoes in food processor or blender along with garlic, basil, parsley, capers, anchovies, Worcestershire and Tabasco. Process, adding some of the reserved soaking liquid, until mixture is a smooth, thick paste. Blend in olive oil. Taste; add pepper and salt as needed. Serve at once, or refrigerate.

3. Serve at room temperature with crusty bread or raw vegetable crudités.

Make Ahead

Cooled cheesecake can be wrapped and frozen for up to 2 months.

Smoked Salmon Cheesecake

8 to 12 appetizer servings

The microwave version of this wonderful make-ahead dish is in my second cookbook, *The Best of New Wave Cooking*. Both versions are showstoppers, though I prefer the appearance, texture and flavour of this oven-baked version. Be sure to make it at least a day before you plan to serve it to allow time for the flavours to develop and blend.

1 teaspoon butter
2 tablespoon dry breadcrumbs
1 tablespoon grated Swiss cheese
1 teaspoon minced fresh dill
1 tablespoon butter
1/2 cup chopped onion
2 8-ounce (250 g) packages cream cheese, softened
3 medium eggs
1/3 cup grated Swiss cheese
1/4 cup light cream
1/4 teaspoon salt, dash of pepper
6 ounces smoked salmon, chopped
3 tablespoons snipped fresh dill
Sour cream, dill sprigs and red peppercorns to garnish

1. Butter the bottom and sides of a 9-inch springform pan.

2. Combine the first 4 ingredients; sprinkle in prepared pan, coating the bottom and sides with the mixture. Set aside.

3. Sauté onion in 1 tablespoon butter in small skillet or microwave until onion is soft.

4. Place onion mixture, cream cheese, eggs, 1/3 cup Swiss cheese, cream and salt in food processor; process until smooth. Add salmon and dill; pulse until just mixed. The salmon should still be in small chunks in the mixture.

5. Pour mixture into prepared pan. Bake in preheated 325°F oven for 1 hour and 10 minutes, or until the cheesecake is almost set at the centre. Turn off oven; leave cheesecake in oven for 1 hour more. Cool to room temperature before wrapping and refrigerating.

6. At serving time, garnish with dill sprigs and red peppercorns.

Shredded Cheese

4 ounces of cheese yields 1 cup shredded cheese

12 ounces of cheese yields 3 cups shredded cheese

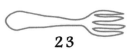

Warm Herb and Spice Olives

Serve this easy Spanish tapas anytime of the year with an assortment of other appetizers, such as salted nuts, grilled sliced Chorizo sausage or a classic Spanish potato omelet.

> 1/4 cup extra virgin olive oil
> 1 minced clove garlic
> 1 tablespoon minced fresh herbs (thyme, rosemary, parsley)
> Dash each, ground cumin and cayenne
> 1 1/4 cups mixed olives (black, stuffed green, etc.)
> Freshly ground black pepper, to taste

1. In small skillet, heat together oil, garlic, herbs and spices.

2. Rinse olives with cold water; pat dry. Add to olive oil mixture in skillet; stir to coat. Heat, stirring often, just until olives are warm. Do not overheat. Serve warm.

Sunshine Fruit Bowl

Serves 6

A healthy, bright and colourful way to start a brunch or to end any meal.
Serve with small, crisp cookies.

8 cups of golden coloured fruit. Choose from:
   Peeled orange sections, membranes removed
   Chopped pineapple
   Peeled, chopped ripe mango and papaya
   Sliced star fruit
   Peeled, sliced bananas
   Slivered dried apricots
   Sliced peaches and nectarines

Gently stir in:
   Sugar, to taste
   A few chopped fresh mint leaves
   Optional fruit liqueur such as Grand Marnier, Triple Sec
       or your favourite fruit liqueur, to taste

Rhubarb Toast Topper

Makes 1 cup

2 cups chopped
rhubarb
2 tablespoons orange
juice concentrate,
undiluted
Brown sugar, to taste

Mix rhubarb
and orange juice
concentrate in small
saucepan. Cook and
stir over medium-low
heat until rhubarb
softens, about 10
minutes. Or heat in
microwave, stirring
often, until rhubarb
is soft. Add brown
sugar to taste.

Optional: add a
few chopped fresh or
defrosted strawberries.
Serve warm or cold.
Refrigerate or freeze
leftovers.

Busy Morning Solutions

To speed up lunch making on busy mornings, wrap and freeze single servings of cookies, muffins, squares, and freezer-friendly sandwiches.
Place in labelled freezer bags and keep handy for quick lunch assembly or handy after-school snacks.

Fruit-Full Orange Bran Muffins

Makes 12 muffins

These moist, chewy muffins, with much more than a hint of orange, will serve you well for breakfast, in a packed lunch or as an after-school snack. They freeze well.

> 1 large seedless orange, washed, chopped
> 2 eggs
> 1/4 cup vegetable oil
> 1/2 cup milk
> 2/3 cup dark brown sugar
> 1 1/2 cups natural bran
> 1 cup all-purpose flour
> 2 teaspoons baking powder
> 1/2 teaspoon baking soda
> Dash of salt
> 1 cup of your favourite dried fruit (or combination): apricots, cranberries, cherries, raisins, dates, blueberries, etc. Substitute chopped nuts for some of the fruit if desired.

1. In food processor, process orange including skin, until very finely chopped. Add eggs, oil, milk and brown sugar; process until well mixed.

2. In medium bowl, stir together bran, flour, baking powder, baking soda and salt. Add orange mixture to flour mixture; stir until just mixed. Stir in dried fruit.

3. Fill 12 lightly greased or paper-lined muffin cups with batter. Bake in preheated 400°F oven for 18 to 20 minutes, or until muffins are firm to the touch on top and nicely browned. These freeze well.

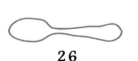

Pumpkin Muffins

Makes 12 muffins

Don't just think of Hallowe'en when you think of pumpkin. It's a tasty and healthy addition to soups, stews, main courses, desserts, and these lovely, spicy muffins.

> 1 1/2 cups all-purpose flour
> 1 tablespoon baking powder
> 1/2 teaspoon each: salt, cinnamon and nutmeg
> 1/3 cup packed brown sugar
> 1 egg
> 3/4 cup milk
> 1/2 cup pumpkin purée
> 1/4 cup canola oil
> 1/2 cup either nuts or raisins *(optional)*

1. In large bowl, stir together flour, baking powder, salt, cinnamon, nutmeg and brown sugar. In smaller bowl, mix together egg, milk, pumpkin and oil. Add liquid mixture to dry mixture; stir just enough to mix. Do not overmix. Stir in nuts and raisins if using.

2. Spoon batter into 12 greased or paper-lined muffin cups. Bake in preheated 400°F oven for 20 to 25 minutes or until tops spring back when touched.

Other ways with pumpkin: Dice and freeze raw pumpkin for soups and stews. Add grated raw pumpkin to meatloaf mixture, meatballs or poultry stuffing.

Toasted pumpkin seeds: Clean but do not wash seeds, removing pulp and fibres. Sprinkle lightly with canola oil and salt. Spread on baking sheet. Roast at 250°F for 30 to 45 minutes, or until crisp and brown. Stir occasionally. Store in an airtight container.

Pumpkin Pointers

Selecting: Choose small sugar pumpkins for baking or cooking; the flesh is less watery and the flavour is better. Wash and dry skin of pumpkin. Remove stem.

Cooking in the microwave: With a sharp knife blade, cut several slashes in skin of pumpkin. Weigh pumpkin. Microwave on High for 6 to 7 minutes *per pound*, or until sharp knife blade penetrates easily into all sides of the pumpkin. When cool enough to handle, cut pumpkin in half, scoop out seeds, remove skin and purée or mash pulp. Freeze in quantities needed for your favourite recipes.

Strawberry Rhubarb Muffins

Makes 12 large muffins

Rosy rhubarb is one of the first fruits of spring. A few weeks later, when the strawberries ripen, I like to make a batch of these lovely muffins to celebrate the beginning of another season in the garden.

    1 cup brown sugar
    1/4 cup vegetable oil
    1 egg
    1 teaspoon vanilla
    1 cup buttermilk or sour milk
    2 1/4 cups all-purpose flour
    1/2 cup rolled oats
    1 teaspoon each: baking soda and baking powder
    1/2 teaspoon salt
    1 cup each: chopped fresh strawberries and rhubarb

1. In medium bowl, stir together sugar, oil, egg, vanilla and buttermilk or sour milk. (To sour milk, add 1 teaspoon vinegar or lemon juice to regular milk. It will curdle almost immediately.)

2. In large bowl, mix together flour, oats, baking soda, baking powder and salt. Add sugar mixture; stir just until moistened. Stir in fruit.

3. Spoon batter in greased or paper-lined large muffin tin. Bake in preheated 400°F oven for 18 to 20 minutes or until muffin tops are brown and feel firm when touched. Cool in pan 10 minutes before serving. These freeze well for up to 1 month.

Vegetable Confetti Mini Muffins

Makes about 30 mini or 12 regular muffins

These will be a lunchtime lifesaver if you have a "sandwich hater" in your family. Leanne and I made these on a "back-to-school" show one September. They proved to be quite popular with adult viewers as well.

1 1/2 cups all-purpose flour
1/4 cup rolled oats
1 tablespoon sugar
2 teaspoons baking powder
1/2 teaspoon each: chili powder and salt
1/2 cup shredded sharp cheddar cheese
1/4 cup each: finely diced celery, red bell pepper,
　　green bell pepper, and shredded carrot
1 green onion, minced
1 egg, beaten
3/4 cup milk
1/2 cup plain low-fat yogurt or light sour cream
1/3 cup vegetable oil

1. In large bowl, stir together flour, oats, sugar, baking powder, seasonings, cheese and vegetables.

2. In medium bowl, stir egg, milk, yogurt and oil together until well mixed. Add to flour mixture; stir just until dry ingredients are moistened. Do not overmix.

3. Spoon into lightly greased or paper-lined mini or regular muffin pans. For mini muffins, bake in preheated 400°F oven for 12 to 15 minutes, or until browned. For regular muffins, bake in preheated 375°F oven for 20 minutes or until browned.

Variations
　　Add 1/2 cup diced, cooked ham or 4 slices cooked, crumbled bacon to dry ingredients.

Cool It!

To keep packed lunches cool:

Freeze drink boxes, yogurt or applesauce containers.

Freeze cubed melon in small containers.

Freeze small bottles of water.

Freeze sandwiches (that freeze well) overnight or longer; add to lunch bag frozen.

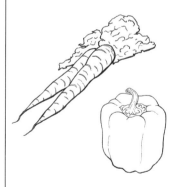

29

Mexican Coffee

For each serving, stir equal amounts of strong hot coffee and hot chocolate in mugs. Top with a dollop of sweetened whipped cream or hot frothed milk and a dusting of ground cinnamon.

Apple Pecan Strata

Serves 8 to 10

Let this spicy, fragrant and delicious dish be the main attraction at your next fall or winter brunch. Because you assemble and refrigerate it the night before, you can relax over coffee with your guests while the strata bakes.

12 cups cubed French bread (1-inch cubes)
2 large apples, peeled, thinly sliced
8 eggs
1/2 cup dark brown sugar
3 1/2 cups light cream or homogenized milk
1/2 cup maple syrup
1 teaspoon cinnamon
1/4 teaspoon nutmeg
1 1/2 teaspoons granulated sugar mixed with 1/4 teaspoon cinnamon
1 cup pecan halves

1. Sprinkle bread cubes and chopped apple in lightly buttered 13 x 9-inch baking pan. In large bowl, whisk together eggs and brown sugar until smooth. Whisk in milk, syrup, cinnamon and nutmeg. Pour evenly over bread and apples. Cover with plastic wrap; refrigerate overnight.

2. Next morning: Remove strata from refrigerator and, if time permits, let stand at room temperature for 1/2 hour. Preheat oven to 350°F. Sprinkle granulated sugar/cinnamon mixture and pecans evenly on top. Cover pan with buttered foil, buttered side down. Bake for 30 minutes; remove foil and bake for 15 to 20 minutes more, or until puffed and golden.

3. Just before serving, dust top with icing sugar or drizzle with warm maple syrup.

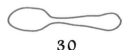

Berry Delicious Fruit Shake

Makes 2 servings

Even very young children can chop bananas to help make these shakes for their friends and family members. Using frozen fruit will make your shake even thicker.

> 8 frozen strawberries or 20 frozen raspberries
> 1 cup fruit juice: orange, pineapple, mango, peach or your favourite
> 1 peeled fresh or frozen banana
> 1 1/2 cups vanilla ice cream or frozen yogurt
> 2 tablespoons chocolate syrup *(optional)*

1. With adult help, place fruit, juice, banana, ice cream and chocolate syrup in blender or food processor. Process mixture until smooth.

2. Garnish glasses with orange slice or fresh berry.

To Make Your Shake Even Yummier

Add one or more of these ingredients:

- smooth or crunchy peanut butter
- plain or chocolate milk
- chopped carrot
- other fruit such as blueberries, mango chunks, peach slices or peeled, ripe pear
- ice cubes
- skim milk powder

Hot Cross Buns
Makes 16

Divide dough into
16 pieces. Shape each
piece into a ball, then
flatten into a round.
Place on greased or
parchment-lined
baking sheet.
Cover and let rise for
30 to 40 minutes.
Brush with egg white.
Using a very sharp
knife, cut a cross in the
top of the bun. Bake in
preheated 375°F oven
for 15 to 20 minutes,
or until puffed and
brown. Cool on racks.

Hot Cross Bunnies
Makes 12 to 16

If you don't have a breadmaker, use homemade or purchased bread dough to make these sweet little bunnies. They make cute decorations for your Easter brunch table.

1/2 cup warm water
1/2 cup low-fat milk
1/4 cup vegetable oil
2 eggs
1/2 cup mixed fruit or peel
1/2 cup raisins or currants
4 cups all-purpose flour
1/3 cup sugar
1 teaspoon salt
1 teaspoon cinnamon
1/2 teaspoon nutmeg
2 teaspoons bread machine yeast
1 beaten egg white
Currants for eyes

1. Measure all ingredients except beaten egg and currant eyes into bread maker in order given or order recommended by the manufacturer of your bread maker. Set to Dough cycle. Press start.

2. When cycle is finished, remove dough from bread pan and knead a few times on a lightly floured surface. Divide dough into 12 to 16 equal dough balls. Divide each ball into 5 pieces: one large ball for body; smaller ball for head and 3 small balls for long, pointed ears and round fluffy tail. Attach the pieces together to form bunnies using beaten egg white. Set bunnies on greased or parchment-lined baking sheets. Cover with tea towels and let rise 30 to 40 minutes, or until doubled in size.

3. Preheat oven to 375°F. Brush bunnies with beaten egg white. Attach currant eyes. Bake for 12 to 15 minutes, or until bunnies are nicely browned. Cool on rack.

Once the bunnies have cooled to room temperature, you can add icing decorations if you wish.

Pancake Initials

If you're really hungry, make pancake letters for your whole name!

> 1 1/4 cups flour
> 2 1/4 teaspoons baking powder
> 1/4 teaspoon salt
> 2 tablespoons sugar
> 1 egg
> 1 1/4 cups milk
> 2 tablespoons melted butter
> 1 tablespoon shortening or oil
> Syrup, jam or applesauce

1. In medium bowl, combine flour, baking powder, salt and sugar. In small bowl, stir together egg and milk until well mixed. Add to flour mixture.

2. Melt butter in saucepan or in microwave. Add to batter; stir with whisk until smooth.

3. Melt shortening in medium skillet over medium heat. Tilt pan to coat bottom with melted shortening.

4. Pour batter into squeeze bottle. Put lid on bottle. Invert bottle over skillet. Squeeze bottle gently and move it to form the letter or shape you want. Pancakes are ready to turn over when the tops are no longer shiny and are covered with bubbles. The edges will be dry and slightly browned. Turn pancakes over carefully with a spatula. Cook other side briefly.

5. Repeat procedure until all batter is used up. As pancakes finish cooking, keep them warm on a plate in a 200°F oven.

6. Serve pancakes with syrup, jam, applesauce or your favourite topping.

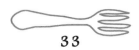

Wrap and Roll:
Quick Bites for Kids in a Hurry

Tortilla Rolls
Spread flour tortillas with your choice of peanut butter, cream cheese, cheese spread or jam. Top with chopped banana, chopped dried fruit, granola or your favourite topping. Roll up and eat, on the run if necessary!

Quick "Egg Roll"
Arrange chopped hard-cooked egg in line in centre of a large flour tortilla. Add salsa, ketchup, mayo or your favourite egg topping. Sprinkle with pepper and shredded cheese. Roll up, tucking in ends to form a bundle. Microwave on High for 30 to 40 seconds or until hot. Serve at once.

Vegetable Wraps or Pockets
Spread large plain or flavoured flour tortillas or inside of pita bread halves with your favourite spread. Sprinkle with your choice of chopped fresh vegetables such as cucumber, peppers, lettuce, celery, tomatoes, etc. Add minced herbs, sprouts, freshly ground pepper, shredded cheese, sliced ham or chicken, or your choice of fillings. Roll tortillas or close pita halves.

Pizza Rolls
Place one or more small flour tortillas on a baking sheet (for oven) or microwave-safe plate(s). Spread with a thin layer of pizza sauce and some shredded mozzarella cheese. Add toppings of choice: e.g. chopped pepperoni, chopped green pepper, sliced mushrooms. To cook in the oven, place under the broiler until cheese melts and bubbles. To cook in the microwave, microwave 1 tortilla at a time on High for 1 minute, or until cheese melts and bubbles. Cool for a few minutes, then roll up and eat.

Family Sub

Makes 4 to 6 servings

The fun begins when everyone in the family helps assemble supper.

    1 baguette
    Butter, mustard, mayonnaise or ketchup
    Sliced deli meats: ham, salami, smoked turkey, your choice
    Sliced cheese: cheddar, mozzarella, your choice
    1 tomato, thinly sliced
    Cucumber slices
    Red and green pepper slices
    Shredded lettuce
    Oregano and pepper, to taste

1. With adult help, cut bread in half lengthwise. Spread both pieces of bread with your choice of butter, mustard, mayonnaise or ketchup.

2. On one side, layer your choice of filling ingredients—meats, cheeses, vegetables. Top with shredded lettuce and a sprinkling of oregano and pepper.

3. Close sandwich, securing with toothpicks if necessary. Cut it into serving-size pieces.

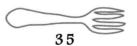

Crunchy Chicken Fingers

Makes 3 to 4 servings

Everyone in the family will enjoy these for lunch or dinner.

3 cups cornflakes
1/4 cup cornmeal
1/2 teaspoon garlic salt
1/2 teaspoon dried oregano
1/4 teaspoon salt
1/4 teaspoon pepper
3 tablespoons butter, melted
2 tablespoons oil
2 whole boneless chicken breasts, cut into strips
(or use fillets leftover from another recipe)
Dipping sauces: barbecue, plum, teriyaki or your favourite.

1. Place cornflakes in heavy plastic bag; crush with rolling pin. Add cornmeal, garlic salt, oregano, salt and pepper to cornflake crumbs. Shake bag to mix well.

2. Combine melted butter and oil in flat bowl or pie plate.

3. Dip chicken pieces in butter mixture to coat, then place in bag with crumb mixture. Shake to coat chicken pieces well with crumbs. Shake off excess crumbs. Arrange chicken pieces on lightly greased baking sheet.

4. Bake in preheated 350°F oven for 15 minutes, or until chicken is brown and crisp. Cut into 1 piece to see if it is fully cooked. It should be white all the way through, with no traces of pink remaining.

5. Serve chicken fingers with your favourite dipping sauces.

Cupcake Cones

Makes 18 to 20 cones

Invite your friends over for a baking party. Let guests decorate their own cones, then serve them with fruit shakes for a yummy snack.

> 1 single layer cake mix, prepared according to package directions
> 18 to 20 flat-bottom ice cream cones
> 1 cup frosting, purchased or homemade
> Candy sprinkles, chopped dried fruit, nuts or coconut

1. Spoon 2 heaping tablespoons of cake batter into each cone. Place filled cones on a baking sheet, or place 6 at a time in a circle in the microwave.

2. **Oven:** Bake in preheated 350°F oven for 20 minutes, or until toothpick inserted into centre comes out clean.

   Microwave: Microwave 6 cones at a time on High for 1 1/2 to 3 minutes, or until a toothpick inserted into centre comes out clean. Repeat with remaining cones until all are baked.

3. Cool cones completely. When cool, spread tops with frosting and decorate with sprinkles, fruit, nuts or coconut. Use your imagination!

All-Day Beef Stew

Serves 6

Make-Ahead Safety Tip

To prepare the night before: Chop and refrigerate beef, vegetables, seasonings and stock **separately**.

Assemble in pot in the morning, just before cooking.

Like the All-Day Pot Roast in *PamCooks,* this is a wonderfully fragrant and comforting dinner to come home to after a busy winter day.

1 1/2 pounds cubed lean beef (inside or outside round, sirloin tip, stewing beef, etc.)
1 medium onion, chopped
4 large carrots, peeled, sliced
2 potatoes, peeled, chopped
2 parsnips, peeled, chopped
2 cups peeled chopped rutabaga
1 tablespoon olive oil
3 cups beef stock or more
1/2 cup tomato juice or dry red wine
1/2 teaspoon each: dried thyme and oregano
1 bay leaf
Salt and pepper, to taste
1 cup chopped green beans or peas
1/3 cup cornstarch dissolved in 1/4 cup cold water

1. **To cook the stew**: Combine beef and chopped vegetables (those listed above or your choice) in large Dutch oven or casserole. (Do not add beans or peas at this point.) Drizzle with olive oil; stir well.

2. Stir in beef stock, tomato juice or wine, and seasonings. Add more beef stock or water, enough to completely cover vegetables. Cover pot; place in a 200°F oven. Cook for 6 to 10 hours. Stew will be cooked after 6 hours but can continue cooking for up to 4 more hours if desired.

3. **To finish the stew**: Add beans or peas and remove bay leaf. Stir in cornstarch mixture. Heat and stir in microwave or on stovetop over low heat until thickened. Taste and adjust seasonings.

4. Serve with crusty bread, scones or Cheddar Herb Dumplings *(recipe on next page).*

Cheddar Herb Dumplings

Serves 6

One mouthful of these and I'm transported back to my childhood dinner table and my Mom's fluffy dumplings atop a steaming bowl of her rich beef stew.

> 1 1/2 cups all-purpose flour
> 1 tablespoon minced fresh parsley
> 1 teaspoon minced fresh herbs (thyme, rosemary, savory, dill, etc.)
>   or 1/2 teaspoon dried
> 2 teaspoons baking powder
> 1 teaspoon salt
> 1/4 teaspoon pepper
> Dash cayenne
> 1/2 cup shredded sharp cheddar cheese
> 2/3 cup milk
> 1 egg
> 2 tablespoons olive or vegetable oil

1. In medium bowl, stir together all dry ingredients including cheese. In small bowl, combine milk, egg and oil; add to flour mixture. Stir just until flour is incorporated. Do not overmix or dumplings will be tough.

2. **If cooking in microwave:** Drop spoonfuls of dumpling mixture onto hot bubbling stew in circle around edge of casserole. Cover and microwave on High for 5 to 7 minutes, or until dumplings are completely cooked. Let stand for 3 minutes before uncovering and serving.

   If cooking on stovetop: Heat stew over low heat until bubbly. Drop spoonfuls of dumpling mixture onto stew; cover pan. Cook over lowest heat setting for 15 to 20 minutes, or until dumplings are fully cooked.

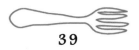

Variation

Replace beef with chicken or pork. Cook until well done and no longer pink inside.

Beef Saté with Peanut Sauce   Serves 6

These work well as appetizers, or as the main attraction when served with vegetables and rice or noodles.

> 1/2 cup dark soy sauce
> 1/4 cup dry sherry
> 1 tablespoon brown sugar
> 2 cloves garlic, crushed
> 1 1/2 pounds lean boneless beef steak
> Peanut Sauce *(recipe on next page)*

1. Cut beef into 1-inch cubes; place in a medium bowl.

2. Mix soy sauce, sherry, sugar and garlic; pour over meat. Toss to coat. Marinate at room temperature for 30 minutes.

3. Remove meat from marinade and thread onto bamboo skewers, allowing 1 to 2 skewers per person. Broil or grill for 7 to 10 minutes, or until cooked to taste. Turn occasionally and baste with marinade during the first half of cooking time. Serve hot or at room temperature, with hot basmati or jasmine rice. Garnish with cilantro or parsley sprigs.

Peanut Sauce

Makes 1 cup

A must with saté. If you don't have time to make it from scratch, prepared versions are available in most supermarkets.

>   2 tablespoons minced onion
>   3 cloves garlic, crushed
>   1/4 to 1/2 teaspoon red pepper flakes
>   1/4 teaspoon ground coriander
>   1/2 tablespoon chopped lemon grass
>   2/3 cup coconut milk
>   1/4 cup chunky peanut butter
>   1/2 tablespoon brown sugar

1. Purée onion, garlic, pepper flakes, coriander and lemon grass in a blender, food processor or mortar and pestle until mixture forms a smooth paste.

2. Place mixture in a small skillet and cook over low heat for 3 to 4 minutes. Stir constantly.

Lemon Grass

At first glance, lemon grass looks a bit like a green onion, but is tougher and more fibrous. Choose lemon grass with greenish leaves rather than yellow, and with a base that is firm and not dried out. The bulbous base is used whole to infuse flavour to sauces and soups, and is usually removed before the dish is served. Sometimes it is thinly sliced and ground together with herbs and spices to make curry pastes. The long leaves can be chopped and used in tea, either fresh or dried. Lemon grass can be frozen; use more if frozen to get the same flavour intensity as fresh. If you cannot find lemon grass at your supermarket, substitute lemon or lime zest and juice.

Cook for One You're Worth It!

Try these small-quantity recipes, found elsewhere in this book:

- Quick Bites, *page 34*
- Shrimp and Avocado Salad, *page 76*
- Pesto Broiled Tomatoes, *page 85*
- Grilled Vegetable Packets, *page 89*
- Greek-Style Grilled Chicken, *page 50*
- Coquilles St. Jacques, *page 56*
- Ginger Lime Salmon in Parchment, *page 60*
- Egg and Veggie Wrap, *page 67*
- Spring Vegetable Omelet, *page 68*
- Vegetable and Cheese Frittata, *page 69*
- Orange Mini Cheesecake, *page 109*
- Biscuit Tortoni in Chocolate Cups, *page 121*

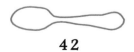

One-Rib Prime Rib Roast

Serves 2 to 4

This recipe for singles is the wonderful creation of my mother Dorothy Searles who loves to cook, much to the delight of her neighbours and family who are often the recipients of her delicious soups and sweets.

> 1 1-rib prime rib roast, about 1 1/2 pounds
> Dijon mustard
> Freshly ground pepper, to taste

1. Look for a 1-rib roast, or ask your butcher to cut one for you. It will probably be about 1 1/2 pounds and 1 1/2-inches thick. Wrap roast and place in freezer until solidly frozen.

2. Coat surface of still-frozen roast with mustard; sprinkle with pepper. Place in roasting pan. Roast at 325°F for about 1 1/2 hours or until meat thermometer registers 140°F for rare. If roast is slightly larger, it will take longer to cook. Plan on 2 hours for a 2-pound roast.

3. From this roast, you should have one main meal, enough leftovers for hot and cold sandwiches for a day or two, and a pot of soup if you make stock from the bone.

Grilled Herbed Lamb Chops

4 servings

A summer favourite in our house! If you're going camping, freeze chops in marinade in heavy freezer bags. They will defrost and be ready to grill by the time the tent is pitched.

    1 large clove garlic, minced
    1/4 cup balsamic vinegar
    3 tablespoons olive oil
    1/2 teaspoon dried mint, crumbled
    1/2 teaspoon dried rosemary leaves, crumbled
    1/4 teaspoon coarsely ground pepper
    8 loin lamb chops

1. Combine marinade ingredients; pour over chops set in glass baking pan. Cover, refrigerate and marinate for 4 hours, turning chops over occasionally.

2. Grill over hot coals 4 to 6 minutes per side, or until cooked to desired degree of doneness.

A Brush with Thyme (or Rosemary!)

Use sprigs of thyme or rosemary as basting brushes when grilling meat or poultry.

When you dry rosemary, thyme or any other herbs with woody stems, remove the leaves from the stems, then save the stems to toss in the fireplace or woodstove next winter.

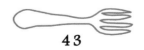

How to "Butterfly"

Cut a lengthwise slit in the pork tenderloin from one end to the other, almost all the way through. Open up, like a book. Flatten the meat between 2 sheets of plastic wrap.

Cider-Glazed Pork Tenderloin with Caramelized Onion and Apple Stuffing

6 servings

CJOH-TV viewer Helene Seguin tried this recipe and "everyone thought it was simply delicious!" The perfect dish for autumn dinner parties or Sunday dinner for the family.

1 Spanish onion, chopped
2 tablespoons olive oil
1 teaspoon brown sugar
2 tart apples, peeled, chopped
1/4 cup dried cranberries
1 tablespoon chopped fresh sage (*1 teaspoon dried*)
2 tablespoons balsamic vinegar
Salt and pepper, to taste
2 large or 3 small pork tenderloins, butterflied
1 to 2 cups apple cider
1/3 cup whipping cream
Salt and pepper, to taste

1. In large skillet, sauté onion in olive oil over medium-low heat until tender and lightly browned, 30 to 40 minutes. Stir often. Stir in sugar, apples, cranberries, sage and balsamic vinegar; cook 5 to 8 minutes more, or until apples just begin to soften. Season lightly with salt and pepper.

2. Flatten butterflied tenderloins between 2 sheets of plastic wrap. Spoon some of the onion apple stuffing onto each tenderloin. Roll up to enclose filling. Tie with twine at 1 1/2-inch intervals. Brush with olive oil. Place seam-side down in baking pan along with remaining stuffing. Roast at 350°F for 15 minutes. Pour cider into pan around meat. Roast for 30 to 45 minutes more, or until meat thermometer registers 160°F. Baste occasionally with pan juices and add more cider if needed.

3. Remove tenderloins and stuffing from pan and keep warm. Add cream into pan juices, stir to mix. Heat gently until hot.

4. Slice tenderloins; arrange slices on warm serving platter. Drizzle sauce over. Garnish with sprigs of fresh sage or parsley.

5. Serve with Two-Potato Purée *(page 87)* and Vegetable Medley with Dill Lemon Mayonnaise *(page 90).*

Chopped Onions

1 small onion equals 1/3 to 1/2 cup chopped onion

1 medium onion: 3/4 to 1 cup chopped

1 large onion: 1 1/2 cups or more

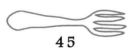

Instant Read Thermometer

- A handy kitchen tool with several uses:
- To help you determine when meat and poultry is cooked to a safe and healthy degree of doneness.
- To ensure that you don't overcook roasts and steaks if you like them rare.
- To make sure that hot water and scalded milk used in breadmaking is the correct temperature to react with the yeast.

For accurate measurement, leave thermometer in for 1 minute before taking the reading.
Makes a great Christmas stocking stuffer or shower gift!

Maple Mustard Pork Tenderloin

Serves 4

A quick and tasty entrée to grill in summer and oven roast when the weather is cold.

> 1/4 cup maple syrup
> 2 tablespoons Dijon mustard
> 1 clove garlic, crushed
> 1/2 teaspoon dried thyme
> Freshly ground pepper, to taste
> 2 pork tenderloins, about 3/4 pound each

1. In small bowl combine all ingredients except pork. Coat tenderloins on all sides with mustard mixture. Place tenderloins in a glass pan, cover with plastic wrap and marinate in refrigerator for 1 to 4 hours.

2. Grill on a medium-hot barbecue or roast in a 350°F oven until internal temperature of pork at thickest point reaches 160°F.

3. Slice thinly and serve.

More Maple Magic: A Maple Orange Glaze for Ham

In small bowl stir together 1/4 cup orange marmalade, 1 tablespoon maple syrup and 1/2 tablespoon Dijon mustard. Spread over ham one hour before it finishes baking.

Chicken Asparagus Packets

Serves 4

These packets can be oven baked if you choose not to grill them. Change the vegetables from season to season, to suit your tastes.

    4 boneless skinless chicken breasts
    Salt and pepper, to taste
    Minced fresh herbs of choice: tarragon, basil, thyme, rosemary,
        parsley, chives, etc.
    8 teaspoons dry white wine or chicken stock
    4 stalks asparagus, thinly sliced diagonally
    2 carrots, peeled, cut into thin julienne strips
    1/4 cup chopped green onion or chives
    4 24-inch pieces foil, doubled (or 4 12-inch pieces of heavy foil)

1. Sprinkle each chicken breast half with salt and pepper. Place in centre of heavy or double foil. Sprinkle each chicken breast with one fourth of the herbs and 2 teaspoons wine or chicken stock. Top with asparagus, julienne strips of carrot and minced green onion or chives.

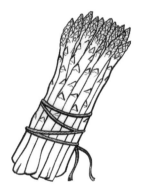

2. Seal packets well, crimping edges so that no steam can escape. Place on hot grill. Cook on high heat for 10 to 15 minutes, turning over frequently, until package puffs up, indicating that chicken is fully cooked. (To check, cut into the thickest part of chicken to ensure that no pink colour remains.)

   Regular oven: Bake packets in preheated 400°F oven for 25 to 30 minutes, or until packets puffs up and chicken is cooked through. No pink colour should remain when you cut into the thickest part of the piece.

3. Just before serving, sprinkle contents of packet with minced fresh parsley.

Coq Au Vin Blanc

Serves 6

Viewer Carrol Mooney served Coq au Vin Blanc to dinner guests and wrote: "Over the years I have got a lot of good recipes from your CJOH-TV cooking segment and this one tops the list! I don't think I have ever cooked anything that left such a nice aroma in the house."

3 slices bacon, diced
6 serving pieces of chicken *(boneless skinless thighs
    and breasts are best)*
1 cup chopped onion
2 cloves garlic, minced
12 ounces fresh mushrooms, cleaned, quartered
2 carrots, peeled, cut into bite-sized pieces
1/2 teaspoon Herbes de Provence
    (see page 54, Provençal Turkey Breast)
1/2 teaspoon salt
1/4 teaspoon pepper
1/4 cup flour
1 cup dry white wine
1 1/2 cups chicken stock
1 bay leaf

1. In large skillet, cook bacon until crisp. Remove from pan. In same pan, brown chicken pieces. Remove from pan.

2. If no pan drippings remain, add 1 tablespoon oil to same skillet. Sauté onion, carrots and garlic over medium heat until onion is softened. Add mushrooms, herbs and seasonings; cook and stir until liquid from mushrooms evaporates.

3. Add flour; cook and stir for 1 minute. Whisk in wine and stock. Add bay leaf. When mixture boils, return chicken and bacon to pan. Spoon liquid over chicken pieces. Cover pan, turn heat to low and simmer for 30 minutes, or until chicken is fully cooked and sauce is thickened.

For oven baking: After browning chicken, transfer to large casserole dish. Prepare vegetables and sauce as in Steps 2 and 3 above, then pour mixture and bacon over chicken. Cover casserole and bake at 350°F for 30 minutes. Uncover casserole and bake for 20 minutes more. Remove bay leaf.

4. Garnish with minced fresh parsley before serving. Can be cooked a day ahead and reheated at serving time.

Serving Suggestions

- Garlic mashed potatoes, or buttered wide noodles tossed with poppy seeds or toasted walnuts
- Green salad with radicchio, blood orange segments and red onion slivers
- Steamed asparagus with browned butter and shaved Parmesan cheese, or crumbled chèvre

Greek-Style Grilled Chicken

Serves 2 as main course or 4 in salad

This is one of my favourite ways to grill chicken. Serve it with vegetables as the main attraction, tuck it into a sandwich or cut it into strips and add it to a seasonal salad.

2 boneless skinless chicken breast halves, flattened between sheets of plastic wrap

Marinade:

1/4 cup olive oil
Juice of 1/2 large lemon
1/2 teaspoon dried oregano
1 crushed clove garlic
Salt and freshly ground pepper, to taste

1. Combine marinade ingredients in large flat dish. Add chicken, turning to coat both sides with marinade. Cover and refrigerate 2 hours or overnight.

2. Grill until browned and fully cooked. Serve hot or cold.

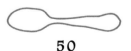

Summer Salad with Grilled Chicken and Strawberries

Serves 4

Vinaigrette:

> 2 tablespoons raspberry or other fruit vinegar
> 1/4 cup olive oil
> 1/2 teaspoon Dijon mustard
> Salt and pepper, to taste

Salad:

> Large bowl mixed greens, washed, torn into bite-sized pieces
> 1 to 2 cups sliced strawberries
> 1/2 cup toasted slivered almonds
> 1 recipe Greek-Style Grilled Chicken (or your favourite grilled chicken recipe)
> Optional ingredients: roasted pepper strips, grated carrot, chopped tomatoes, chopped cucumber, etc.

1. Measure vinaigrette ingredients into a jar with a tight-fitting lid; set aside.

2. At serving time: In edible bread bowl *(page 78)* or regular salad bowl, toss greens, most of the strawberries and most of the almonds with enough vinaigrette to moisten. Arrange chicken strips, remaining berries and almonds on greens. Serve at once.

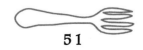

Quick Mexican Chicken

Serves 4

This family-friendly dish can be assembled and in the oven in less than 10 minutes—just what you need at the end of a busy day.

> 1/2 teaspoon chili powder
> Dash each: ground cumin and salt
> 4 boneless skinless chicken breast halves
> 4 slices Monterey Jack cheese
> 1 1/2 cups salsa

1. In small bowl, combine chili powder, cumin and salt. Sprinkle evenly over chicken. Place chicken in a lightly oiled baking dish large enough to hold chicken in a single layer.

2. Top each chicken breast with a slice of cheese. Pour salsa over all.

3. Bake in preheated 375°F oven for 25 to 30 minutes, or until chicken is completely cooked. Check by cutting into thickest part of 1 piece; chicken meat should be white, not pink.

4. Serve with rice flavoured with minced red and green pepper, frozen or canned corn and chopped parsley or cilantro.

Slow Cooker Cassoulet

Serves 4

Traditional cassoulet takes hours, even days, to assemble. The flavour is wonderful, but most of us don't have that kind of time. This slow cooker version is a satisfying and delicious alternative.

1/2 pound boneless skinless chicken breast or thigh meat,
cut into 1-inch chunks
Salt and pepper, to taste
1/2 cup chopped onion
1 carrot, diced
1 medium tomato, seeded, chopped
1/4 cup chopped fresh parsley
1 clove garlic, minced
1/2 teaspoon each: salt, thyme and rosemary
1/4 teaspoon pepper
4 cups cooked white navy beans, or 2 19-ounce (540 mL) tins white
beans, drained and rinsed
1/2 pound smoked sausage, cut into bite-sized pieces
1/2 cup chicken or beef stock
1/4 cup dry white wine
1 bay leaf

1. Place all ingredients in slow cooker. Stir gently to mix. Cover and cook on Low for 5 to 6 hours, or until chicken is cooked through and flavours have blended. Stir occasionally if possible.

2. Remove bay leaf before serving. Serve with crusty bread and a green salad.

Herbes de Provence

A mixture of the most common herbs used in cooking in Provence in the south of France. It usually includes basil, fennel seed, lavender, marjoram, rosemary, sage, summer savory, and thyme, or a combination of several of these herbs. It can be found already prepared in bulk food stores, specialty stores and bottled with the spices in your supermarket.

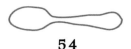

Provençal Turkey Breast

Serves 6

If there are leftovers, slice thinly for sandwiches, casseroles, salads, or as a topping for pizza.

> 1 1/2 pounds boneless, skinless turkey breast
> Herbes de Provence *(see sidebar)*
> 2 tablespoons olive oil or butter
> 1/2 cup dry white wine
> 2 tablespoons balsamic vinegar
> Salt and pepper, to taste

1. Coat both sides of turkey breast with herbs. Heat oil or butter in large heavy skillet. Brown turkey well on both sides over medium-high heat.

2. Turn heat to low. Pour wine and vinegar around turkey. Cover skillet; simmer gently until turkey is fully cooked (no pink colour remains when you cut into the centre) and liquid is thickened, about 1/2 hour.

3. To serve, slice thinly and arrange on platter. Drizzle pan juices over.

Mexican Lasagna

Serves 8 to 10

When I mentioned to Leanne that I was going to do this book, her first reaction was, "You have to include the Mexican Lasagna." This is a quicker simpler version of a recipe given to me by Kathy Black of Ottawa. It's great for parties or potlucks.

  1 1/2 pounds ground turkey or lean ground beef, crumbled
  1 medium onion, chopped
  2 cloves garlic, minced
  3 1/2 cups extra chunky salsa
  Freshly ground pepper
  1 container (475–500 g) light cottage cheese or light ricotta
  1 egg
  1/4 cup minced fresh parsley
  2 cups shredded Monterey Jack cheese, divided
  12 to 15 small flour tortillas
  1 medium tomato, seeded, diced
  Chili powder
  Optional toppings: Shredded lettuce, chopped green onions,
      sliced black olives, guacamole, etc.

1. In large skillet, cook turkey, onion and garlic over medium heat until meat is no longer pink. Stir in salsa. Heat to boiling. Season lightly with pepper.

2. In medium bowl, stir together cottage cheese, egg, parsley and 1 cup of the Jack cheese.

3. To assemble, lightly grease or spray the bottom and sides of a 13 x 9-inch baking pan. Cover bottom and sides with a layer of tortillas. Spoon in turkey mixture in an even layer. Cover with a layer of tortillas. Top with cottage cheese mixture in an even layer. Sprinkle diced tomato and remaining cheese evenly on top. Sprinkle lightly with chili powder. Cover and refrigerate at this point if desired.

4. Bake at 350°F for 30 to 45 minutes, or until hot and bubbly. Let stand 5 minutes before cutting into squares. Let each person garnish with the toppings of their choice.

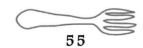

Coquilles St. Jacques

2 servings

Read and I usually start our New Year's Eve Dinner for Two with this classic dish. The recipe easily doubles or triples for entertaining.

1/2 cup dry white wine
1/4 cup water
Juice of 1/2 lemon
1/4 pound scallops
1/4 pound shrimp, shelled, deveined
1/2 cup chopped fresh mushrooms
1 tablespoon butter
2 green onions
1 1/2 tablespoons flour
Salt, pepper, cayenne, to taste
1/2 cup reserved cooking liquid *(step 1 below)*
1 tablespoon minced fresh parsley
1/4 cup cream

1. Combine wine, water and lemon juice in small saucepan. Bring to a boil. Add scallops, shrimp and mushrooms; simmer 5 minutes. Drain, reserving 1/2 cup of the cooking liquid.

2. Melt butter in small saucepan over medium heat. Add green onions; cook until soft. Remove from heat.

3. Stir in flour and seasonings to taste; mix well. Gradually whisk in reserved cooking liquid, blending until smooth. Return to heat; cook and stir until mixture thickens. Stir in cream, scallops, shrimp, mushrooms and parsley. Stir gently to blend.

4. Spoon mixture into 2 buttered scallop shells or small gratin dishes. Can be prepared ahead to this point, covered and refrigerated for several hours.

5. Bake in preheated 400°F oven for 10 to 15 minutes, or until bubbly and lightly browned.

Shrimp, Chicken and Pineapple Kebobs

Serves 4

A taste of the tropics that makes dinner taste like summer, no matter what the season.

> 1/2 cup dark soy sauce
> 1/4 cup pineapple juice
> 2 large cloves garlic, crushed
> 1 tablespoon brown sugar
> 16 large shrimp, shelled, deveined
> 1 pound boneless skinless chicken breast, cut into 1-inch cubes
> 3 cups cubed fresh pineapple (1-inch cubes)

1. Mix soy sauce, pineapple juice, garlic and brown sugar. Pour half over shrimp in one bowl and half over chicken cubes in another. Toss to coat. Marinate at room temperature for 30 minutes. Refrigerate if marinating time is longer.

2. Remove shrimp and chicken from marinade. Thread onto bamboo skewers, alternating shrimp and pineapple on half of the skewers and chicken and pineapple on remaining skewers. Broil or grill for 10 to 15 minutes, or until fully cooked. Turn occasionally and baste with marinade during first half of cooking only.

3. Serve with Tropical Fruit Salsa *(see sidebar)*, rice pilaf and grilled vegetables.

Tropical Fruit Salsa

Makes about 2 cups

- 1 ripe mango, peeled, chopped
- 1 cup each, chopped ripe papaya and pineapple
- 3 green onions, finely chopped
- 1 to 2 jalapeno peppers (to taste), minced
- 2 tablespoons each, chopped fresh mint and cilantro
- Zest and juice of 1 large lime, or more, to taste
- Salt, to taste

Combine all ingredients in medium bowl. Stir gently to mix. Cover and refrigerate. Before serving, taste and adjust flavourings, if needed.

Southeast Asian Curried Shrimp with Vegetables

4 servings

Don't be put off by the lengthy ingredient list. Half of them are used to make the curry paste that gives this dish a fresh and fabulous curry flavour that's well worth the time it takes to make it.

2 large cloves garlic
1/2 cup chopped onion
2 tablespoons chopped lemon grass
2 tablespoons lime juice
2 teaspoons paprika
1 teaspoon ground turmeric
1 1/2 teaspoons brown sugar
1/2 teaspoon ground cinnamon
1/4 teaspoon allspice
1/4 to 1/2 teaspoon red pepper flakes
1 1/2 tablespoons vegetable oil
1/2 teaspoon sesame oil *(optional)*
12 ounces shelled and deveined shrimp
1 cup broccoli flowerets, green beans or chopped asparagus
1 cup thinly sliced carrots
1/2 cup slivered red pepper
1 cup coconut milk
1/4 cup water
1 tablespoon fish sauce or soy sauce
2 teaspoons cornstarch
Fresh parsley or coriander, to garnish

1. **Curry Paste**: In food processor or using mortar and pestle, purée garlic, onion, lemon grass, lime juice, paprika, turmeric, brown sugar, cinnamon, allspice and red pepper flakes until smooth. Let stand for 1 hour to blend flavours if possible.

2. Heat both oils in wok. Add curry paste; cook and stir over medium-high heat for 2 minutes, or until mixture is bubbly and fragrant. Add shrimp; stir to coat shrimp with curry paste.

3. Stir in vegetables and coconut milk; cook and stir for 3 to 5 minutes, until vegetables are tender and shrimp is cooked.

4. In small bowl, mix together water, fish sauce and cornstarch. Add to wok; cook and stir until mixture boils and thickens. Spoon hot mixture over cooked rice. Serve with sliced cucumbers.

Ginger Lime Salmon in Parchment

Serves 2

Steam-cooking fish in parchment or foil results in fish that is moist and flavourful. Make one packet just for you, or multiply ingredients for entertaining.

> 2 salmon fillets or steaks, 4 to 6 ounces each
> 2 teaspoons vegetable oil
> Salt and pepper, to taste
> Zest and juice of 1 lime
> 2 teaspoons chopped fresh ginger
> 1 1/2 tablespoons chopped green onion
> Dash salt
> 1/4 of a red bell pepper, finely chopped
> 1 whole lime, sliced
> Butter

1. Pat salmon dry with paper towels. Rub small amount of oil on both sides of fish. Sprinkle lightly with salt and pepper; set aside.

2. **Ginger mixture**: Finely mince together lime zest, ginger, green onion and a dash of salt. Divide into 2 equal portions; set aside.

3. **For each serving**: Cut a piece of parchment to approximately 12 x 10 inches. Lightly butter or oil an area the size of the pieces of salmon in the centre of the parchment. Sprinkle 1/4 of the ginger mixture on buttered area. Top with salmon; sprinkle the juice of 1/2 lime on each piece of salmon. Top with remaining ginger mixture, red pepper and 1 lime slice.

4. Fold parchment over salmon, and seal packages so that no steam can escape during cooking. *(Can prepare ahead and refrigerate for several hours at this point.)*

5. Put packages on baking sheets; bake in preheated 500°F oven for 8 minutes per inch of thickness of salmon.

6. Serve salmon in parchment or remove it before serving. Serve with wild and white rice, or a grain and vegetable pilaf, and steamed broccoli, asparagus or snow peas.

How to Choose and Store Fresh Fish

Whole fish should have firm, shiny skin, bright red gills and bright, clear eyes. Fish steaks and fillets should look and smell fresh, and should be moist with no dry looking areas. Fresh fish doesn't smell "fishy," like ammonia. Fish should be cooked the day you purchase it, but will usually keep for a day or two. Store it in the coldest part of the refrigerator, wrapped well, and ideally, packed in ice. Live shellfish should be kept in refrigerator in ventilated containers or bags with no added water.

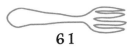

Two for the Grill

Grilled Tilapia

Serves 4

Canadians are finally "discovering" this delicious, firm, white-fleshed fish that's been farmed and enjoyed around the world since ancient Egyptian times.

>1/4 cup olive oil
>2 tablespoons fresh lemon juice
>1 clove garlic, crushed
>1/4 teaspoon dried oregano leaves
>Freshly ground pepper, to taste
>4 tilapia fillets

1. Combine all ingredients except tilapia in small bowl. Place tilapia fillets in glass dish large enough to hold it in a single layer. Pour marinade over fillets; turning to coat both sides of fish with marinade. Let stand at room temperature for 30 minutes. Refrigerate if marinating for a longer time.

2. Place tilapia in well-oiled grill basket. Grill for 3 to 5 minutes per side, or until fish flakes easily with a fork.

Seafood Grilled on a Cedar Plank

A fun way to add fish to your barbecue menu. Be sure to purchase wood planks that haven't been treated with chemicals.

> Salmon steaks or fillets, or your favourite fish fillets
> Large scallops or shrimp
> Freshly ground pepper
> Toppings: your choice of lemon juice, maple syrup or mayonnaise
> flavoured with dill, grainy Dijon mustard and lemon

1. Preheat grill to hot (400°F).

2. Place items to be grilled on untreated cedar planks. (If desired, planks may be soaked in water for 30 minutes before grilling. This is not essential.) Place planks on grill and have a spray bottle of water handy. Close the lid of the barbecue and lower heat setting to medium.

3. Grill seafood for 10 minutes per inch of thickness of fish, measured at thickest part. Check often and extinguish flames when edges of planks begin to burn. Salmon is cooked when it is opaque and flakes easily with a fork. Scallops are cooked when they are opaque.

4. As soon as fish is cooked, drizzle with maple syrup and lemon juice, or top with a dollop of dill mayonnaise.

Dessert Suggestion

A light, fruity dessert would nicely finish this meal. Make a Mexican-style fruit salad by combining a selection of several of the following: chopped melon (any type), pineapple, mango, papaya, strawberries, bananas and oranges. Add chopped fresh mint, lime juice and sugar to taste.

Mexican Macaroni and Cheese   Serves 6

My daughter Amy insisted that this recipe be included. It's one of her favourite comfort foods—mine too.

> 2 1/2 cups whole wheat rotini, macaroni or other small pasta
> 2 tablespoons butter or oil
> 1 small onion, chopped
> 1 clove garlic, minced
> 1/4 cup flour
> 1 teaspoon each: salt and chili powder
> 1/2 teaspoon each: pepper and ground cumin
> 3 cups milk
> 2 1/2 cups grated Monterey Jack cheese
> 1 4.5-ounce (127 mL) tin chopped green chilies, drained
> Toppings: 1/4 cup crushed tortilla chips and 1/4 cup shredded
>   Monterey Jack cheese, chili powder

1. Cook pasta in large pot of boiling, salted water until tender. Drain and set aside.

2. Melt butter in large saucepan or microwave-safe casserole. Add onion; sauté until onion is soft but not brown. Stir in garlic; cook 1 minute more, either on stovetop or in microwave on High.

3. Add flour, salt, chili powder, pepper and cumin; mix well. Slowly whisk in milk. Cook and stir over medium heat (whisk several times if cooking in microwave) until sauce becomes hot and thick. Remove from heat; stir in cheese and chilies. Continue stirring until cheese melts and sauce is smooth.

4. Add cooked pasta to sauce; mix well. Spoon into buttered 11 x 7-inch casserole or baking pan. Sprinkle toppings over mixture. Bake in preheated 375°F oven for 30 minutes, or until toppings are nicely browned and casserole is bubbly.

5. Serve with your favourite marinated tomato, cucumber and bell pepper salad.

Swiss Raclette for Four

An easy party meal that comes together quickly after a day of skating or cross-country skiing.

> 1 pound raclette cheese (substitute French Port Salut or Italian Fontina)
> 1 jar sour gherkins
> 1 jar small white pickled onions
> 12 to 15 small new potatoes, scrubbed, boiled, kept warm
> French bread
> 1 pound thinly sliced good quality smoked ham

Cheese is held close to heat source *(see below)* until surface melts. Melted portion is then scraped onto dinner plates and served with new potatoes, sour gherkins, pickled onions, ham and bread. Cheese is then placed close to heat source again, to melt the next layer. Salads may also be served, if desired.

Raclette stoves can be rented or purchased.

Raclette Cooking Methods

Fireplace: Toast a large wedge of cheese on a long fork held close to fire, or build a makeshift platform of bricks or blocks. Use a cast-iron griddle to hold cheese.

Toaster oven: Place it as close to the table as possible. Set cheese slices on greased or sprayed shallow pan. Use high heat or Broil setting to melt cheese.

Regular oven: Set oven to 350°F. Place 1/2-inch thick cheese slices on ovenproof plates or greased baking sheet. Bake for 7 to 9 minutes, or until cheese melts.

Broiler: Broil on greased or sprayed baking sheets until cheese melts.

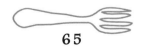

Asparagus Cheese Soufflé

Serves 3 to 4

Don't Be Intimidated!

Don't be afraid to attempt a soufflé. Success will be yours if you carefully follow each step in the recipe. It is a good idea to prepare and measure all ingredients before you begin to cook. To serve your soufflé, two forks work better than a spoon. Insert the tines of the forks together into the top of the soufflé, then separate them as you cut down into the soufflé, dividing it into portion-sized pieces.

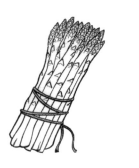

Make sure diners are at the table when the soufflé is ready. Even as it is carried from oven to table, it begins to deflate.

Butter
2 tablespoons grated Parmesan cheese (1st amount)
2 cups diced asparagus
Salt and pepper
2 tablespoons butter
3 tablespoons flour
1 cup hot milk
1/2 cup grated Parmesan cheese (2nd amount)
4 egg yolks, lightly beaten
Salt and pepper
6 egg whites, whipped until stiff

1. Coat inside of a 6-cup soufflé dish with butter. Sprinkle with 2 tablespoons Parmesan. Rotate dish to coat bottom and sides with cheese. Set aside. Preheat oven to 400°F.

2. Steam asparagus in small amount of water until tender. Sprinkle with salt and pepper. Drain well. Set aside.

3. In medium saucepan or microwave-safe dish, melt 2 tablespoons butter. Whisk in flour. Slowly whisk in hot milk. Cook and stir for 2 minutes (or microwave on High, whisking every minute) until sauce thickens. Stir in asparagus and 1/2 cup Parmesan; cook and stir just until mixture boils.

4. Remove from heat. Whisk a small amount of the asparagus mixture into the egg yolks to warm them. Stir warm yolk mixture into asparagus mixture. Sprinkle lightly with salt and pepper. Cool slightly.

5. Fold asparagus mixture and beaten whites together carefully until no streaks of yellow remain. Pour into prepared soufflé dish. Bake in preheated oven for 35 minutes, or until puffed and golden. Serve at once.

Eggs-cellent Dinners for One or Two

Egg and Veggie Wrap
Serves 1

My daughter Amy perfected this healthy fast-food supper. These wraps look especially pretty made with flavoured red or green tortillas.

> 1/2 teaspoon oil
> 1 green onion, chopped
> 2 tablespoons each: chopped red and green peppers and chopped spinach leaves
> 1 large mushroom, thinly sliced
> 1/2 of an Italian plum tomato, seeded, chopped
> 1 egg, beaten
> Salt, pepper and dried oregano or basil
> 1 to 2 tablespoons shredded cheese
> 1 large spinach or other flavoured flour tortillas, warmed in oven or microwave

1. In small (7-inch) non-stick skillet, cook vegetables in oil over medium heat until tender; transfer to small bowl.

2. Pour beaten egg into same pan; rotate to coat pan bottom with egg. As soon as egg begins to set, top with vegetable mixture, a light sprinkle of salt, pepper and oregano, and cheese; cook until egg is set.

3. Slide cooked egg onto tortilla; roll tortilla tightly around egg. Secure with a toothpick.

Quick Egg Fajita
Serves 1

Prepare egg with vegetables as described at left, omitting spinach, tomato and cheese. When fully cooked, cut egg into strips. Pile strips onto a warm flour tortilla and garnish with your choice of salsa, chopped tomato, shredded lettuce, guacamole, shredded cheese, sour cream, etc. Roll up, tucking in bottom edge to keep filling from falling out.

Spring Vegetable Omelet

Serves 1

2 teaspoons butter
1 cup (approximately) sliced asparagus spears
3 or 4 wild leeks (ramps), white part only,
    or 1 green onion, thinly sliced
1 egg plus 2 egg whites (or 2 eggs), beaten
Salt and pepper
1/3 cup shredded cheese (cheddar, chèvre, Swiss, your choice)

1. Melt butter in 7-inch non-stick skillet. Sauté asparagus and leeks or onions until tender. Transfer to bowl and keep warm.

2. Heat same skillet until hot. Pour in egg; rotate pan to coat bottom and sides with egg. As eggs cook, lift edges with spatula or knife so that liquid egg runs under cooked egg. As soon as egg is almost fully cooked, sprinkle with salt and pepper. When omelet is cooked to taste, spoon vegetable mixture onto half of omelet. Top with cheese. Fold other half of omelet over vegetables and cheese. Slide omelet onto warm dinner plate and serve at once.

Vegetable and Cheese Frittata

Serves 2

1 teaspoon olive oil
1 small onion, chopped
1 small clove garlic, minced
1 small potato, baked, peeled sliced
1 to 2 cups chopped or sliced vegetables (bell peppers, mushrooms,
    broccoli, celery, etc.)
1 slice ham, finely chopped *(optional)*
Dash of pepper and dried oregano
3 eggs, beaten with 1 tablespoon water or milk and a dash of salt
1/2 cup shredded or crumbled cheese (cheddar, chèvre, Swiss,
    mozzarella, etc.)
1 tablespoon freshly grated Parmesan *(optional)*
Minced fresh parsley and basil, if available
Salsa to garnish, if desired

1. Heat oil in medium skillet. Add all vegetables; cook over medium heat,
   stirring occasionally, until vegetables are soft. Season with pepper and
   oregano.

2. Turn heat to low. Pour egg mixture evenly over vegetables. Cover pan and
   cook gently until eggs are set. Sprinkle cheese over. Cover and let stand
   until cheese melts. Serve hot.

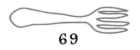

Vegetable and Cheese Torta   Makes 6 to 8 servings

A rainbow of colourful layers tucked inside a golden puff pastry shell. Serve it at your next vegetarian dinner party or brunch. Add a layer of sliced smoked ham for a non-vegetarian version.

1 package purchased puff pastry, defrosted overnight in the
   refrigerator
1 tablespoon oil
1 tablespoon butter
2 tablespoons pine nuts or chopped walnuts
1/2 cup chopped onion
1 10-ounce bag of spinach, stems removed
1 clove garlic, minced
1/2 teaspoon ground nutmeg
Salt and pepper
2 red peppers, roasted, peeled, sliced
1 1/2 cups (6 ounces) thinly sliced cheese (provolone, Swiss,
   mozzarella, cheddar, your choice) cheese, thinly sliced
2 7-inch omelets, each made with 3 eggs, seasoned with minced
   chives, parsley and other fresh herbs of choice, salt and pepper
Egg wash: 1 egg, beaten with 1 teaspoon water

1. Lightly grease an 8-inch springform pan. Roll out three-quarters of the pastry on a lightly floured board to 1/4-inch thick. Line bottom and sides of pan with pastry. Roll remaining pastry to make an 8-inch circle for the top. Refrigerate pan and top separately.

2. Heat oil and butter in large skillet. Add pine nuts; cook and stir over medium heat until nuts are toasted. Use a slotted spoon to transfer nuts to a small dish.

3. Add onions; cook and stir until onions soften. Turn heat to high. Add spinach and garlic; cook and stir on high heat for 3 minutes, or until spinach wilts. Drain off excess moisture. Chop spinach (scissors work well for this). Add nutmeg, salt and pepper to taste. Stir in pine nuts; set aside.

4. Prepare and assemble remaining ingredients as indicated. Layer ingredients in pastry-lined pan in following order: 1 omelet, half of the spinach, half of the cheese, all of the red pepper, the remaining cheese, remaining spinach and the second omelet. Set top crust on torta; trim and seal edges. Brush top with egg wash.

5. Bake in preheated 350°F oven for 1 hour and 15 minutes, or until golden brown. Cool 10 minutes in pan. Release sides of pan and transfer to serving plate. Use a very sharp thin-blade knife to slice into wedges. Serve warm.

Raspberry Vinegar

Bring 2 cups white wine vinegar and 1 cup fresh raspberries to boil. Remove from heat; transfer to glass bowl. Cover; refrigerate overnight. Strain through fine sieve lined with several layers of cheesecloth into sterilized bottles. Seal and store in dark, cool place. Makes 2 cups.

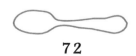

Green Salad with Pears, Chèvre and Sugared Pecans

8 servings

A simple green salad made memorable with the addition of sweet, crunchy pecans, soft, ripe pears and smooth, tangy chèvre.

Washed mixed salad greens, including spinach and radicchio
1/2 cup pecan halves
2 teaspoons butter
Sugar
Vinaigrette *(recipe follows, or use your favourite vinaigrette)*
2 ripe pears, sliced
1 3-ounce package soft goat cheese (chèvre) crumbled

Raspberry Vinaigrette:

3 tablespoons raspberry or cranberry vinegar *(recipe in sidebar)*
1 tablespoon orange juice
1/2 cup olive oil
2 tablespoons walnut or hazelnut oil *(optional)*
1/2 teaspoon Dijon mustard
Salt and pepper, to taste

1. Wash greens; tear into bite-sized pieces. Place in plastic bag and chill until serving time.

2. **To prepare pecans:** Melt butter in small skillet until foamy. Stir in pecans; cook and stir until pecans are toasted and fragrant. Sprinkle with sugar to coat; cook 1 minute more. Transfer to bowl; set aside until serving time. Can be prepared a day ahead.

3. **Vinaigrette:** In jar with a tight-fitting lid, shake together all vinaigrette ingredients. Taste and adjust flavours. Refrigerate until serving time.

4. **To serve:** Arrange greens on individual salad plates. Top with sliced pears, crumbled chèvre and pecans. Drizzle salads lightly with a small amount of vinaigrette (refrigerate leftover vinaigrette). Serve at once.

Marinated Carrot Salad with Fresh Dill

Makes 4 to 6 servings

A brief blanching enhances the colour and texture of the carrots in this make-ahead salad. Enjoy leftovers for lunch the next day.

1 pound carrots, peeled, cut in thin julienne strips (3 1/2 cups)
1 1/2 tablespoons raspberry or white wine vinegar *(see page 72)*
1/4 cup olive oil or vegetable oil
1 tablespoon minced fresh parsley, dill and chives or green onions
1 small clove garlic, minced
1/4 teaspoon salt
Freshly ground pepper

1. Blanch carrots in boiling water for 2 minutes, or until crisp-tender and bright. Place cooked carrots in ice water as soon as cooking is done, to refresh them and to stop further cooking.

2. Combine vinegar, oil, parsley, dill, onions, garlic, salt and pepper in a jar with a tight-fitting lid; shake well to blend. Taste and adjust seasonings.

3. Pour dressing over carrots and mix well. Refrigerate at least 4 hours before serving. Can be made a day ahead.

Carrot Companions

Many different herbs, spices and flavours enhance and complement the taste of carrots, including allspice, bay leaves, caraway, cloves, cumin, ginger, garlic, mustard, maple, lemon, orange, dill, curry, cinnamon, rosemary, mint, parsley and basil. Try something new the next time you serve carrots.

Decorate with Herb Blossoms

All herb blossoms are edible. Nibble first to determine whether their flavour suits the dish you will use them in. Sprinkle into salads, sauces and dips, or use to garnish vegetable dishes, cheese or pâté, serving platters or dinner plates. Chive and garlic chive blossoms or other larger herb blossoms can be torn into flowerets before using. Blossoms of herbs such as borage, basil, bergamot, summer savory, sage and sweet cicely are just a few you might want to try.

Potluck Pointers

- If you are planning a potluck, indicate to those attending how many servings of their dish they should bring.
- If cooking and reheating facilities are at a premium, suggest that food be brought hot, or that dishes that are served cold would be suitable.
- If you are bringing food to a potluck, take along all utensils and dishes needed to serve your food. The host may not have what you need.
- A list of ingredients is a good idea, especially if your dish includes items that some guests might be allergic to, such as shellfish, peanuts, hazelnuts, dairy, etc.

Red Cabbage Salad

Serves 12

Take this colourful salad to a potluck supper and you won't have to worry about leftovers. Don't be intimidated by the long list of ingredients. The salad can be assembled quite quickly and can be made a day ahead.

1/2 cup vegetable oil
1/2 cup sugar
3/4 cup cider vinegar
2 teaspoons dry mustard
1 1/2 teaspoons celery seed
1 teaspoon salt
1/2 teaspoon pepper
1 minced clove garlic
1 head red cabbage, shredded
4 green onions, minced
2 carrots, peeled, shredded
1 red and 1 green pepper, chopped
1 tin corn niblets, drained
1/2 cup chopped fresh parsley
1/4 cup minced fresh dill *(optional)*

1. In medium saucepan, bring oil, sugar and cider vinegar to boil; boil 5 minutes. Stir in celery seed, mustard, salt, pepper and garlic. Set aside to cool.

2. In large bowl, mix all remaining ingredients together. Pour oil mixture over all; mix well. Taste and add more seasonings as needed. Cover and refrigerate 4 hours or overnight before serving.

Salade Niçoise

Serves 4

The perfect summer picnic lunch, and so simple to prepare.

Salad:

6 cups mixed salad greens
Minced fresh herbs: basil, chives, parsley, etc.
1 pound or more tiny new potatoes, scrubbed, cooked, cooled,
 quartered or sliced
3/4 pound green beans, trimmed, steamed until crisp-tender, cooled
2 ripe tomatoes, cut into wedges
2 7-ounce (198 g) tins water-packed solid white tuna, drained
 (or, if available, 1 pound fresh grilled tuna is delicious in this
 recipe)
Garnish: black olives, capers, slivered red onion, drained
 and rinsed anchovies *(optional)*, more herbs

Vinaigrette:

1/4 cup extra virgin olive oil
2 tablespoons balsamic or red wine vinegar
1/2 teaspoon grainy Dijon mustard
1 large clove roasted garlic *(see page 96)*
Salt and pepper, to taste

1. Arrange a bed of greens on each of 4 dinner plates. Sprinkle lightly with herbs of choice.

2. Arrange potatoes, beans, tomatoes and tuna attractively on each plate.

3. Purée vinaigrette ingredients together in small food processor or blender. (Or mash roasted garlic and add remaining ingredients, whisking until smooth.) Taste and adjust seasonings.

4. Drizzle vinaigrette over salads. Add your choice of garnishes. Serve with crusty whole-grain rolls.

Chive Ribbons

Blanch long chives for a few seconds in boiling water, pat dry, then use to tie serving-size bundles of green beans, julienne carrots or asparagus stalks, or to secure filo pastry beggars' purses.

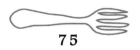

Choosing an Avocado

A ripe avocado will be dark but not black, heavy for its size and quite firm. It should barely dent when you squeeze it gently. Avoid those that are very black and soft to the touch. They are overripe and will probably be inedible. If you purchase bright green avocadoes that are not yet ripe, keep in mind that they may take up to a week to ripen. Store avocadoes at room temperature. After cutting, the flesh will darken and discolour quickly unless you brush the cut surface with lemon or lime juice. Pressing plastic wrap directly onto the surface of cut or mashed avocado will also slow discoloration.

Shrimp and Avocado Salad

Serves 2

A classic combination that never goes out of style. The perfect starter for a romantic dinner for two.

> 4 to 5 large cooked shrimp per person, shelled, deveined, chilled
> 4 cherry tomatoes, quartered
> 1/4 cup diced English cucumber
> 1 tablespoon each, minced fresh parsley and dill
> 1/2 teaspoon finely minced onion
> 1 large ripe avocado, peeled, diced
> Salad greens for two, in bite-sized pieces

Vinaigrette:
> 2 tablespoons olive oil
> 2 teaspoons white wine vinegar
> 1 teaspoon balsamic vinegar
> Dash of Dijon mustard
> Salt and pepper, to taste

1. In large bowl, combine shrimp, tomatoes, cucumber, parsley, dill and onion. Gently stir in avocado.

2. Measure vinaigrette ingredients into small bowl. Whisk to mix well. Taste and adjust seasonings.

3. **To serve:** Arrange a bed of salad greens on each of 2 salad plates. Gently toss shrimp mixture with vinaigrette; spoon onto greens and serve. (Or omit greens and mound salad in avocado shells.)

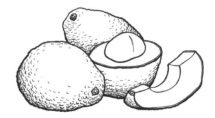

Spinach Salad with Hazelnut-Crusted Chèvre and Clementine Garnish

4 servings

A lovely and attractive salad to serve at holiday parties in December and all through the winter, when citrus fruit is in abundance. Conveniently, ready-to-serve baby spinach leaves can now be purchased in bulk in whatever quantity you require.

Salad:

> 3 ounce package of soft goat cheese
> Olive oil
> 1/4 cup ground hazelnuts or filberts
> Large bowl of washed baby spinach leaves and one small head of radicchio, in bite-sized pieces
> Slivered red or green onion, to taste
> 2 or 3 clementines or oranges, peeled, separated into segments

Cranberry Vinaigrette:

> 2 tablespoons cranberry vinegar
> 1/2 tablespoon orange juice
> 1/4 cup olive oil
> 1 tablespoons hazelnut or walnut oil
> 1/4 teaspoon Dijon mustard
> Salt and pepper, to taste

1. Cut cheese into 4 equal pieces. Shape each piece into a round. Coat each piece with olive oil, then roll in ground nuts to coat. Set aside.

2. Wash spinach and radicchio. Place in salad bowl or plastic bag; chill until serving time.

3. In jar with a tight-fitting lid, shake together all vinaigrette ingredients. Taste and adjust seasonings; set aside.

4. At serving time, heat cheese in microwave on Medium for 30 to 60 seconds, or place in moderate oven for 5 minutes, until hot and soft. Toss greens and orange segments with enough vinaigrette to coat. Spoon salad onto individual salad plates; top each serving with a portion of goat cheese. Serve at once.

Cranberry Vinegar

Makes 4 cups

Combine in glass bowl 1 bag fresh or frozen cranberries, 4 cups white wine vinegar and 1/3 cup raisins. Press fruit to crush it. Allow to steep for at least 24 hours. Strain through layered cheesecloth or coffee filter. Add sugar to taste. Pour into clean bottles. Add a few fresh or frozen cranberries to bottle before sealing if desired. Store in cool dark place.

Mixing and Proofing without Food Processor or Microwave:

Mix dough by hand, adding enough water to make a smooth ball. Knead by hand for 8 to 10 minutes or until smooth. Place in oiled bowl and cover with cloth. Let rise 30 minutes or until almost doubled in bulk. Dough is now ready to roll.

Bread Bowl

Nibble vinaigrette-soaked morsels of this edible bowl along with the salad you've served in it. No dishes to wash! Thanks to chef Cindy Yabar for showing me how to make this yummy bowl.

1 ball of your favourite purchased pizza dough, breadmaker bread dough or this homemade pizza dough:
   2 2/3 cups flour
   2 teaspoons instant yeast
   1 teaspoon Italian seasoning
   2 tablespoons olive oil
   1 cup or less warm water (120–130°F)

1. **To make dough**: Measure dry ingredients into food processor. Pulse to mix. Add oil; pulse again. With food processor running, slowly pour water through feed tube until a ball forms (do not add remaining water once this happens). Continue to process for 1 minute.

2. **To proof in microwave**: Remove dough and blade from work bowl. Shape dough into a ball; make a hole in the centre and place dough ring over stem in work bowl. Cover bowl with plastic wrap. Place in microwave with 1 cup water. Microwave on lowest power level 3 minutes; let stand 3 minutes. Microwave on lowest power level for 3 more minutes; let stand for 6 minutes. Dough is now ready to roll.

3. Generously oil the outside of a large ovenproof bowl. Set the bowl upside down on an oiled baking sheet. Set aside.

4. Roll dough on a lightly floured surface to a circle large enough to cover bowl. Place dough over bowl and smooth the surface. Trim and crimp edges.

5. Bake in a preheated 350°F oven for 25 to 30 minutes or until nicely browned. Cool on bowl for 15 minutes before removing.

Tabouleh with a Twist

Makes 6 to 8 servings

Add your choice of chopped seasonal vegetables, beans, grains and lentils to make tabouleh that suits your tastes.

         1 1/2 cups water
         1 cup bulgur
         1 1/2 teaspoons salt
         1/4 cup fresh lemon juice
         1/2 to 1 teaspoon minced fresh garlic
         1 cup cooked brown or wild rice
         1/2 cup chopped green onion
         1 tablespoon chopped fresh mint *(1 teaspoon dried)*
         1/3 cup olive oil
         1 cup cooked chickpeas
         1/2 cup diced cucumber
         1/3 cup each: diced red and green pepper
         2 medium ripe tomatoes, diced
         1 cup minced fresh parsley
         Freshly ground pepper and salt, to taste

1. Bring water to boil in microwave or in pot on stove. Add bulgur and salt; let stand for 20 minutes, or until bulgur is chewable and all water is absorbed.

2. Add lemon juice, garlic, rice, onion and mint; mix well. Refrigerate for 2 to 3 hours to blend flavours.

3. At serving time, add remaining ingredients and mix well. Taste and adjust seasonings, including lemon juice. Serve cold.

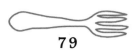

Risotto in the Microwave

Do step 1 in original recipe in large microwave casserole. Transfer vegetable mixture to bowl. Add 2nd amount of butter to casserole; Microwave to melt butter. Stir in rice and wine; cover and microwave on High for 3 minutes or until wine is absorbed. Stir in 2 cups of stock (note: this is the total amount of stock needed for this version). Cover and microwave on High for 5 to 7 minutes, or until stock boils. Stir, cover and microwave on Medium for 12 to 14 minutes, or until liquid is absorbed and rice is tender. Stir in vegetable mixture and remaining ingredients. Microwave on High for 2 minutes, stirring after 1 minute, until mixture is creamy and hot. Serve immediately.

Risotto with Spring Vegetables   Serves 6

This creamy rice entrée can be the main attraction, or a side dish for fish or poultry. It's definitely worth the time it takes to make it.

    2 tablespoons butter (1st amount)
    1/2 cup chopped onion
    2 cloves garlic, minced
    1 1/2 cups sliced asparagus
    1/2 cup each: slivered red and yellow pepper
    2 tablespoons butter (2nd amount)
    1 cup Italian arborio rice (medium grain rice)
    1/2 cup dry white wine
    6 cups chicken or turkey stock
    1/2 cup whipping cream
    1/2 cup freshly grated Parmesan
    1 green onion, chopped
    2 tablespoons minced parsley, dill or basil
    Freshly ground pepper

1. Melt 2 tablespoons butter in large saucepan over medium heat. Stir in chopped onion and garlic; sauté until onion begins to soften. Stir in asparagus and red and yellow peppers; cook until vegetables are crisp-tender and still brightly coloured. Transfer vegetables to bowl. Set aside.

2. Add 2 more tablespoons butter to same pan. Add rice; stir to coat rice with butter. Cook 2 minutes. Add wine; cook and stir until wine is absorbed by rice. Add 1 cup of stock; cook uncovered over medium heat, stirring often, until stock is absorbed. Continue to stir, adding stock one cup at a time, allowing each cup of stock to be absorbed by rice before adding the next cup. Cook and stir until rice is tender and mixture is creamy, 25 to 30 minutes.

3. Stir asparagus mixture into rice, along with remaining ingredients. Serve as soon as vegetables are heated through.

Hazelnut Apricot Rice Ring

Serves 6 to 8

An elegant presentation that's simple and quick and sure to dazzle your guests!

    3 tablespoons butter, divided
    1/2 cup chopped leeks
    1/3 cup chopped dried apricots
    1/4 cup coarsely chopped hazelnuts
    2 1/4 cups basmati or long-grain rice
    4 cups hot chicken stock
    1/4 cup minced fresh parsley
    Salt and pepper, to taste

1. Melt half of the butter in large saucepan; cook leeks over medium heat until soft but not brown. Stir in apricots and hazelnuts; cook for 1 minute more. Add rice; stir to coat with butter.

2. Add stock to rice; bring to boil over high heat. When stock boils, cover pot, turn heat to low and simmer gently for 20 minutes, or until all liquid is absorbed by rice.

3. Stir in parsley and remaining butter. Press firmly into *generously* buttered 6-cup mold. After 1 minute, unmold onto serving platter. Fill centre with vegetables such as cooked carrot coins, steamed broccoli florets or sautéed cherry tomatoes.

Long-Grain White Rice ~ rice grains have been hulled and polished. Use when you want rice grains that are separate, light and fluffy.

Brown Rice ~ still has the hull on, so has more vitamins and fibre than white rice. Texture is chewy when cooked, and flavour is nutty. Longer cooking time than white rice.

Basmati Rice ~ a fragrant, aromatic rice used in Asian cooking. I love the flavour and use basmati rice almost exclusively. When cooked, grains are separate. Jasmine rice, also an aromatic rice, is stickier than basmati when cooked, but similar in flavour.

Italian Arborio Rice ~ medium to short grain rice that cooks to a creamy consistency.

Wild Rice ~ not really rice but a type of grass. More expensive than other types, but with exceptional flavour, texture and nutritive value. Takes longer to cook than other types of rice.

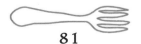

Toppings for Asparagus or Fiddleheads

- **Mustard Cream Sauce:** 1/4 cup light sour cream heated with 2 to 3 teaspoons grainy Dijon mustard

- Melted butter and fresh lemon juice to taste

- Freshly grated Parmesan cheese

- **Easy Hollandaise-Type Sauce:** Stir together and heat 3/4 cup light mayonnaise, 1/4 cup light sour cream, 1 tablespoon fresh lemon juice and 2 teaspoons Dijon mustard. Drizzle over hot asparagus, fiddleheads or broccoli, or use to make Eggs Benedict. Makes about 1 cup.

Grilled Asparagus with Tarragon Vinaigrette

Serves 4

We enjoy asparagus from the garden almost every day when it's in season. When food is fresh, keep the preparation simple for best flavour.

        1 clove garlic
        1/3 cup olive oil
        Salt and pepper, to taste
        1 to 1 1/2 pounds asparagus spears
        8 to 10 cherry tomatoes, halved
        2 hard-cooked eggs, peeled, quartered
        Minced parsley
        Your favourite vinaigrette dressing

1. Crush garlic; mix with olive oil in small bowl. Add a dash of salt and pepper. Set aside.

2. Wash and trim asparagus spears. Pat dry. Preheat grill.

3. Brush spears lightly with garlic oil. Grill until just tender and lightly browned, about 5 minutes. Turn often.

4. Transfer to serving platter. Garnish with cherry tomato halves and egg quarters. Sprinkle with minced parsley. Drizzle with vinaigrette.

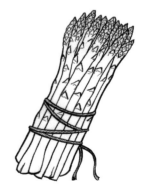

Carrot and Broccoli Stir-Fry

Serves 4 to 6

Serve as a side dish with your favourite Asian entrées, such as Beef Saté on page 40.

    1 tablespoon toasted sesame seeds
    1 teaspoon vegetable oil
    1 teaspoon sesame oil
    1 clove garlic, minced
    1 medium head broccoli, in small florets
    2 cups sliced carrots
    Salt and pepper, to taste

1. In small skillet over medium heat, toast sesame seeds until light brown. Set aside.

2. Heat both oils in large skillet or wok. Add garlic, broccoli and carrots. Stir-fry over medium-high heat until vegetables are tender. Sprinkle with salt and pepper, transfer to serving bowl and sprinkle with sesame seeds before serving.

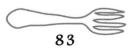

Carrot and Zucchini Sauté

Makes 4 servings

You can never have too many zucchini recipes, because you never know when a canoe-sized zucchini will "materialize" in your garden!

> 1 tablespoon olive oil or butter
> 1 small onion, chopped
> 2 cloves garlic, minced
> 4 cups freshly shredded zucchini
> 2 large carrots, scrubbed, grated
> 2 tablespoons minced fresh herbs of choice (basil, oregano, dill, tarragon, etc.)
> Salt and pepper, to taste

1. In large non-stick skillet, sauté onion and garlic in butter or oil over medium heat until soft but not brown.

2. Increase heat to medium high. Stir in zucchini and carrot. Cook, stirring constantly, just until vegetables are hot and slightly softened. Remove from heat. Stir in herbs, salt and pepper to taste. Serve at once.

Barbecue Method: Wrap entire mixture in heavy foil; seal package well. Grill on barbecue, turning often, until package puffs slightly. Serve at once.

Balsamic Dill Vinaigrette

Purée the following mixture in a food processor:

3 tablespoons olive oil
2 tablespoons minced fresh dill
1 tablespoon balsamic vinegar
1 tablespoon cider vinegar
1 small clove garlic
Salt and pepper, to taste

Drizzle over freshly steamed or chilled green beans, or julienne carrots.

Pesto Broiled Tomatoes

2 servings

A quick and colourful side vegetable for your next dinner party. This recipe can easily be doubled or tripled as needed.

Cut 1 large ripe tomato in half from stem end to blossom end. Trim a thin slice from rounded side so tomato sits firmly on baking dish. Sprinkle cut surface lightly with salt. At serving time, spread homemade or purchased pesto sauce over cut surface to coat. Broil until pesto begins to bubble. Serve warm.

All~Seasons Pesto Sauce

Makes 1 cup

Even though this pesto was included in my previous book, you will want to have it handy for this recipe.

> 1 1/2 tablespoons toasted pine nuts or walnuts
> 1 cup packed spinach leaves, no stems
> 1/4 cup snipped fresh parsley
> 1 clove garlic
> 1 teaspoon dried basil leaves
> 1/4 teaspoon salt
> 1/3 cup olive oil
> 1/3 cup freshly grated Parmesan cheese

1. Place nuts, spinach, parsley, garlic, basil, salt and oil in blender or food processor. Process until smooth.

2. Transfer to bowl. Stir in Parmesan. Taste and add salt and pepper as needed. Will keep in the refrigerator for one week. Freezes well.

Microwave Baked Potatoes

Always pierce potatoes with fork before cooking. Cook on High.

1 medium potato:
3 to 4 minutes, or until tender when pierced with sharp knife

2 potatoes:
6 to 7 minutes

4 potatoes:
9 to 11 minutes; arrange in circle

6 potatoes:
14 to 16 minutes; arrange in circle

One Potato, Two Potatoes...

Grilled Potato Halves   Serves 3 to 6

If you bake the potatoes in the microwave before grilling, they brown and crisp on the barbecue in minutes.

> 3 large baking potatoes, scrubbed
> Herbed oil *(recipe below)*

1. **To make herbed oil:** 1/2 cup olive or vegetable oil mixed in a small jar with 1 crushed clove garlic, chopped fresh basil, oregano, chives, or herbs of choice. Store leftovers in refrigerator for up to 1 week.

2. Pierce skin of potatoes several times with fork or sharp knife. Bake potatoes in oven or in microwave (High for 7 to 9 minutes) until tender. Cut potatoes in half lengthwise.

3. Brush skin and cut surface of potatoes with herbed (or plain) oil. Grill over hot coals until all sides are brown and crisp. Sprinkle with salt and pepper before serving.

Two~Potato Purée

Serves 6 to 8

My husband Read isn't a big sweet potato fan, but he enjoyed the not-so-sweet flavour of this simple side dish.

> 1 1/2 pounds Yukon Gold potatoes, peeled, quartered, baked
>   or boiled
> 2 pounds sweet potatoes, peeled, quartered, baked or boiled
> 3 tablespoons butter
> 2 tablespoons milk, or more as needed
> Dash of freshly grated nutmeg
> Salt and freshly ground pepper, to taste

1. Cook both types of potatoes separately until tender. Mash together with butter and enough milk to moisten to desired texture. Add nutmeg, salt and pepper, to taste.

2. Spoon into serving dish. Best eaten right away but can be covered and refrigerated overnight if desired. Reheat at 350°F for 30 to 45 minutes, or until heated through.

Make~Ahead Mashed Potato Casserole

8 servings

My family would mutiny if I didn't produce these creamy potatoes at every holiday dinner! I'm always happy to oblige, since they can be prepared a day ahead.

> 8 large potatoes, peeled
> 4 cloves garlic, peeled
> Water
> 4 ounces light cream cheese, softened
> 1/2 cup light sour cream
> Salt, pepper, onion salt, to taste
> Milk

1. Cook potatoes and garlic cloves in enough water to cover until tender. Drain well.

2. Mash potatoes, garlic, cream cheese and sour cream together until smooth, adding salt, pepper and onion salt to taste, and enough milk to moisten.

3. Spoon into warm serving bowl. Keep warm in 200°F oven until serving time. Can be made ahead, wrapped and refrigerated overnight. Remove from refrigerator 30 minutes before reheating. Reheat in 300°F oven for 30 to 45 minutes, or in microwave until hot.

Grilled Vegetable Packets

Choose the freshest vegetables in colourful combinations for these packets. Experiment with different mixtures each time you make them. Let picky eaters assemble their own.

> 1 cup prepared vegetables of choice per person: thinly sliced carrots, zucchini, mushrooms, chopped asparagus, tomatoes, peppers, onion or leeks, broccoli, etc.
> Salt and pepper, to taste
> Chopped fresh herbs, such as basil, parsley, chives, oregano, savory or tarragon, to taste
> Your favourite oil and vinegar dressing, to taste
> Freshly grated Parmesan cheese

1. Slice or chop vegetables so that all will take about the same length of time to cook. Thicker, more dense vegetables, such as carrots, should be very thinly sliced to speed up cooking time.

2. Prepare 1 packet per person or 1 large packet if 6 people or less. If making one large packet, place vegetables in centre of a large (24-inch long) piece of heavy foil. Make smaller packets for individual servings. Sprinkle vegetables with salt and pepper, chopped herbs to taste, and a drizzle of oil and vinegar dressing. Seal foil packet well on all sides to ensure that no steam can escape.

3. Place packets on grill and cook, turning over occasionally, until packets puff up—this indicates that vegetables are fully cooked.

4. Remove from grill, open packet and sprinkle with Parmesan. Serve from the packet or transfer to serving bowl and add more Parmesan.

Campsite Bouquet

Take a large, lush bouquet of blooming and non-blooming herbs to the campground when you go on holidays. It will last for several days in a pot of water, beautifying your picnic table and adding fabulous fresh flavour to your camp meals. Bouquets of flowering herbs from your garden make lovely hostess gifts.

Vegetable Medley with
Dill-Lemon Mayonnaise

6 servings

This colourful vegetable mixture was a huge success at Christmas dinner last year. The vegetables can be chopped and the mayonnaise made a day ahead. At dinnertime, you only have to steam the vegetables and toss them with the mayonnaise.

Mayonnaise:
> 1/2 cup light or regular mayonnaise
> 1/4 cup fresh snipped dill
> Salt and pepper, to taste
> 1 teaspoon lemon zest
> 2 teaspoons fresh lemon juice

Vegetables:
> 3 cups cauliflowerets
> 3 cups broccoli flowerets
> 2 large carrots, in thin julienne strips

1. Combine mayonnaise ingredients. Taste and adjust seasonings. Refrigerate until needed.

2. Steam vegetables until crisp-tender; toss gently with mayonnaise. Transfer to serving bowl and serve at once.

Cream of Mushroom and Leek Soup

Serves 6 to 8

One of my favourite comfort foods, combining the sweetness of leeks with the earthiness of exotic mushrooms.

5 cups sliced leeks
3 tablespoons butter
1 clove garlic, crushed
1/2 pound mixed mushrooms, sliced or chopped
1/2 teaspoon minced fresh thyme
1/4 cup flour
Dash each: salt and cayenne
1 1/2 cups chicken stock
3 1/2 cups milk
1 tablespoon sherry or lemon juice
Salt and freshly ground pepper to taste
Parsley sprigs and red pepper slivers, to garnish

1. Wash leeks well under cold running water. Slice white and light green parts thinly.

2. Melt half of the butter in a large saucepan; sauté leeks and garlic over medium heat until tender but not brown. Remove from pan.

3. In same pan, melt remaining butter; sauté mushrooms over medium-high heat until lightly browned and until most of the liquid has evaporated. Stir in thyme. Add flour and a dash of salt and cayenne. Gradually add stock and milk. Cook and stir over medium heat until the mixture thickens and comes to a boil. Add leek mixture and sherry or lemon juice. Season to taste with salt and pepper. Garnish and serve hot.

Leeks: Washing and Trimming

Because the white part of the leek is grown underground, leeks must be carefully washed to remove the dirt trapped between the layers of leaves. If your recipe calls for chopped leeks, trim off the root end and the thick dark tops of the outer leaves (they are too tough to eat, but can be used to flavour stock) then slit the leek in half from top to bottom. Hold under cold running water and separate each layer, removing dirt when you find it. Drain and chop. Chopped leeks freeze well without blanching.

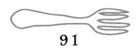

Black Bean and Sausage Soup

Serves 4 to 6

This hearty meal in a bowl tastes even better the next day.

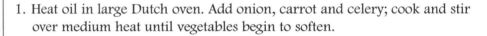

    1 tablespoon vegetable oil
    1 medium onion, chopped
    1 large carrot, peeled or scrubbed, chopped
    1 stalk of celery, sliced
    2 large cloves garlic, minced
    1/2 teaspoon dried oregano
    1 medium potato, peeled, diced
    2 cups beef or chicken broth
    1 28-ounce (796 mL) tin diced tomatoes
    4 to 6 ounces lean kielbasa, cubed
    1 19-ounce (540 mL) tin black beans, or your favourite
        canned beans, drained, rinsed
Salt and freshly ground pepper to taste

1. Heat oil in large Dutch oven. Add onion, carrot and celery; cook and stir over medium heat until vegetables begin to soften.

2. Stir in garlic, oregano, potato, broth and tomatoes; heat to boiling. Stir in kielbasa. Cover and simmer gently for at least 30 minutes to blend flavours.

3. Add beans to soup. Heat until hot. Add salt and pepper to taste. Serve with crusty bread.

Gazpacho

6 servings

The late Peter Gzowski created the original version of this crunchy, slurpy summer soup. I changed it a bit to suit my slightly more timid palate. Make it in August when local tomatoes are at their best.

2 large tomatoes, seeded, chopped
1 large green pepper, chopped
1 to 2 cloves garlic, minced
Chives, parsley, basil, to taste
1/3 cup minced green onion
1/2 English cucumber, chopped
1/3 cup olive oil
Juice of 1 large lemon
1 10-ounce (284 mL) tin beef consommé
1 soup tin of water
1/2 teaspoon salt, or to taste
Pepper, to taste
Sour cream, to garnish

1. Combine all ingredients except sour cream. Cover and chill until cold.

2. Serve garnished with sour cream.

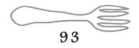

Italian Mussel Soup

4 servings

A heaping bowl of mussel soup, a warm crusty baguette and a glass of chilled Italian white wine is a meal made in heaven, any time of the year.

2 dozen mussels
1/4 cup chopped onion
1 large clove garlic, minced
1 tablespoons butter
2 tablespoons olive oil
1 teaspoon dried basil
1/2 cup dry white wine
1 28-ounce (796 mL) tin diced Italian tomatoes
Juice of 1/2 lemon
Warm French bread

1. Scrub mussels with a stiff brush under cold running water. Discard any mussels that do not close.

2. In large Dutch oven over medium heat, sauté onion and garlic in butter and oil until onion is soft but not brown. Add basil, wine, tomatoes and lemon juice. Heat to boiling.

3. Add mussels to boiling tomato mixture. Cover pot; cook 15 minutes over medium heat. Discard any mussels that do not open after cooking.

4. Ladle mussels and broth into soup bowls. Serve with warm bread.

Roasted Carrot, Onion and Garlic Soup

Serves 4

When carrots are roasted, their flavour becomes intensely rich and sweet, the perfect base for this savoury, smooth soup.

3 tablespoons olive oil
1/2 teaspoon snipped fresh rosemary (1/4 teaspoon dried)
1/4 teaspoon salt and a dash of pepper
2 pounds carrots, peeled, cut into chunks of similar size and shape
2 to 3 large cloves garlic, peeled
1 medium onion, peeled, quartered
6 cups chicken, turkey or vegetable stock

1. Mix oil, rosemary, salt and pepper in large bowl. Add prepared vegetables; stir to coat vegetables with oil. Transfer mixture to lightly greased baking pan. Cover pan with foil. Roast at 400°F for 30 minutes. Remove foil; roast for 30 minutes more or until carrots are almost tender and lightly browned.

2. Heat stock in large saucepan; add vegetables. Simmer for 15 minutes, or until vegetables are very tender. Purée solids in blender or food processor until smooth. Return purée to saucepan.

3. Heat soup until almost boiling. Taste and adjust seasonings. Garnish each serving with a dollop of Parmesan Cream *(see sidebar)* and a sprinkling of minced parsley or chives.

Parmesan Cream Garnish for Soup

1/3 cup whipping cream
2 tablespoons grated Parmesan cheese

Whip cream until stiff. Fold in Parmesan. A delicious garnish for puréed soups.

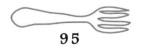

Roasting Garlic

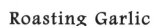

To roast garlic: Trim about 1/4-inch from top of a whole head of garlic. Place on square of double foil. Drizzle lightly with olive oil. Seal foil package tightly. Bake in preheated 350°F oven for 1 hour or until garlic is very soft. When cool enough to handle, squeeze soft garlic out of each clove as needed. Store leftovers in refrigerator for several days or in freezer for several weeks.

Roasted Garlic Vichyssoise

Serves 4

If you've never roasted garlic, give it a try. You'll love its mild flavour in this soup, in mashed potatoes, spread on bread and in a multitude of other dishes.

1 tablespoon butter
1/2 cup chopped leeks
2 tablespoons flour
2 cups chicken stock
2 large potatoes, peeled, chopped
1 or 2 cloves roasted garlic, or more to taste (see sidebar)
1 cup milk, light cream or evaporated low fat milk
Salt and white pepper, to taste
Snipped parsley, to garnish

1. Melt butter in medium saucepan. Add leeks; cook over medium heat until soft. Stir in flour. Slowly stir in stock and potatoes; cover and simmer until potatoes are tender, about 20 minutes.

2. Purée vegetables, including roasted garlic, in food processor or using hand blender, until smooth. Return purée to saucepan with liquid.

3. Stir in milk or cream and seasonings to taste. Heat until very hot but not boiling, or chill and serve cold. Garnish each serving with snipped parsley and herb blossoms, if available.

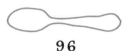

Tortilla Soup

Serves 4 to 6

We tasted this light and lovely soup on our first trip to Mexico. It's one of the many reasons we've vowed to return there as often as possible.

3 soft corn tortillas
Vegetable oil
1/2 cup finely chopped onion
8 cups chicken stock
1/2 cup tomato sauce
1 tablespoon chopped fresh cilantro
Salt, pepper and fresh lime juice, to taste
Sliced lime and chopped cilantro, to garnish

1. Cut tortillas into 1/2-inch strips. Pour enough oil into medium saucepan to cover the bottom of the pan. Heat until hot. Fry tortilla strips quickly for 15 to 30 seconds or until they puff and crisp. Transfer to paper towels to drain. Remove all but 1 tablespoon of oil from saucepan.

2. In same saucepan, sauté onion over medium heat until soft but not brown. Stir in chicken stock and tomato sauce; heat to boiling. Simmer 15 minutes to blend flavours. Stir in cilantro. Add salt, pepper and lime juice to taste.

3. To serve, place some of the fried tortilla strips and a slice of lime in each soup bowl. Ladle soup over. Add more chopped cilantro if desired.

Cilantro or Italian Parsley?

These two herbs are very similar in appearance but very different in flavour. I'm sure that I'm not the only person who has bought one, expecting the other! If you aren't sure which is which in the supermarket, rub a leaf of each between your fingers and smell—you'll soon know the difference!

Wild Rice Soup

6 servings

A truly Canadian way to start a meal. Choose fresh, plump wild rice from Northern Ontario or Manitoba for excellent quality and flavour.

5 cups beef stock
1 tablespoon cornstarch
2 tablespoons butter
1 cup thinly sliced mushrooms
1/2 cup finely chopped carrot
1/2 cup thinly sliced celery
1/2 cup minced onion
2/3 cup wild rice, rinsed with cold water
1/2 teaspoon dried thyme leaves
1 bay leaf
Salt and pepper, to taste
Snipped parsley, to garnish

1. In small bowl, mix one cup of stock with the cornstarch; set aside.

2. Melt butter in large saucepan. Stir in mushrooms, carrot, celery and onion. Sauté over medium heat, stirring often until carrots are tender. Add remaining 4 cups of stock along with wild rice, thyme and bay leaf; bring to boil. Lower heat, cover pot and simmer for 30 to 40 minutes, or until wild rice is tender and vegetables are cooked.

3. Stir cornstarch mixture into soup. Cook over medium heat for 10 minutes or until soup thickens slightly. Stir occasionally.

4. Remove bay leaf. Season to taste with salt and pepper. Garnish each serving with minced fresh parsley.

No-Fail Chocolate Fudge

1 1/2 pounds of fudge

The technique for making this fudge seems strange, but it really does work if you follow directions precisely. Remember—do not stir before cooking in the microwave!

    4 cups icing sugar
    1/2 cup unsweetened cocoa
    3 tablespoons plus 2 teaspoons milk
    1 teaspoon vanilla
    1/2 cup butter
    3/4 cup coarsely chopped nuts

1. Line an 8-inch square baking pan with plastic wrap. Set aside.

2. Mix icing sugar and cocoa together in a large glass casserole. Add milk, vanilla and butter but do not stir. Microwave on High for 3 minutes.

3. Stir in nuts. As soon as fudge begins to visibly thicken, quickly spread in prepared pan. Smooth the top. Chill until firm, then cut into small squares.

Adapted from *The Best of New Wave Cooking* by Pam Collacott (Creative Bound Inc., 1992).

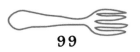

Chunky Oatmeal Cookies with Dates and Walnuts

Makes 4 dozen

With the first crunchy bite, I knew that these would be my new favourite cookie. They're a bit like date squares, but not as sweet and sticky.

1 cup soft butter or shortening
1 cup each: white and brown sugar
2 eggs
2 teaspoons vanilla
2 tablespoons cold water
2 cups all-purpose flour
2 1/2 teaspoons baking powder
1 teaspoon salt
3 cups rolled oats
3/4 cup each: chopped dates and chopped walnuts

1. Cream butter and both sugars together until smooth. Add eggs, vanilla and water; beat until fluffy. Add flour, baking powder and salt all at once; stir until mixed. Stir in oats, then dates and walnuts.

2. Drop by large teaspoonfuls onto greased or parchment-lined baking sheets, leaving 1 inch between cookies. Bake in preheated 325°F oven for 10 to 15 minutes, or until nicely browned. Cool on racks.

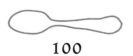

Raisin Spice Cookies

Makes about 2 dozen

I have fond memories of my husband's mother Gwynne whenever I make these. She shared this recipe with me many years ago.

> 1 cup lightly packed brown sugar
> 1/2 cup soft butter
> 1 egg, lightly beaten
> 1/2 teaspoon each: baking soda, baking powder, cinnamon and
>   nutmeg
> 1 1/4 cups all-purpose flour
> Dash salt
> 1 cup raisins

1. Cream brown sugar and butter together in medium bowl. Stir in egg; mix well.

2. Stir dry ingredients together in small bowl; add to sugar mixture. Mix well. Stir in raisins.

3. Drop spoonfuls of dough onto lightly greased or parchment-lined baking sheets. Bake in preheated 375°F oven for 10 to 12 minutes, or until nicely browned.

Perfect Partners

For a lovely "comfort food" dessert, serve Raisin Spice Cookies with warm applesauce and vanilla frozen yogurt sundaes.

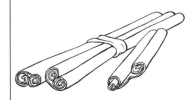

Lemon Squares

Makes about 30 bars

I'm still hearing complaints about last Christmas when I didn't make these. You can't mess with holiday traditions in our house!

Base:
> 1 1/2 cups flour
> 1/3 cup packed brown sugar or 1/2 cup icing sugar
> 3/4 cup cold butter, chopped

Filling:
> 4 eggs
> 1 1/2 cups granulated sugar
> 1 teaspoon baking powder
> Grated zest of 1 large lemon
> 1/2 cup fresh lemon juice

1. **Base:** In food processor work bowl, pulse together flour and sugar to mix. Add butter; process using pulse motion until butter is finely chopped and mixture is crumbly. (Can be done in a mixing bowl using pastry cutter or fingertips to blend.) Press mixture firmly onto bottom of a lightly greased 13 x 9-inch baking pan. Bake in preheated 350°F oven for 15 minutes.

2. **Filling:** In large bowl, whisk eggs and sugar until light. Whisk in baking powder. Stir in lemon zest and juice. Pour over baked base. Bake for 20 to 25 minutes more, or until filling is lightly browned and seems to be set. Cool completely then cut into bars. Store in refrigerator or freezer. Dust with icing sugar just before serving.

Butter Tart Squares

Makes 25 squares

These squares let you enjoy the gooey goodness of butter tarts when you have the craving but not the time to make the real thing.

Base:

>3/4 cup flour
>3 tablespoons packed brown sugar
>1/3 cup cold butter

Filling:

>1 cup packed brown sugar
>3 tablespoons soft butter
>2 eggs
>2 tablespoons flour
>1 cup raisins, chopped nuts or chocolate chips, or a combination of
>>2 or 3 of these

1. **Base:** Stir flour and brown sugar together. Cut in butter using pastry blender or fingertips (or pulse in food processor) until crumbly. Press firmly into lightly buttered 8-inch square baking pan. Bake in preheated 350°F oven for 10 minutes.

2. **Filling:** Cream brown sugar and butter together until smooth. Stir in eggs and flour until smooth. Stir in toppings of choice. Spread mixture evenly over base. Bake for 25 to 30 minutes more, or until golden brown and almost set in the centre. Cool completely before cutting into 25 small squares. Store in a cool place, or freeze.

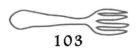

Zucchini Chocolate Brownies

Makes about 48 squares

One of the tastiest ways to eat your vegetables! My mother Dorothy Searles gave me the recipe for this quick and easy snack.

> 3 cups all-purpose flour
> 1/4 cup cocoa
> 1 teaspoon baking soda
> 1 teaspoon cinnamon
> 1/2 teaspoon salt
> 2/3 cup vegetable oil
> 1 3/4 cups sugar
> 2 large eggs
> 3/4 cup plain yogurt
> 1 teaspoon vanilla
> 2 cups shredded zucchini
> 2/3 cup chopped walnuts or pecans
> 1/2 cup chocolate chips

1. Lightly grease a 13 x 9-inch baking pan. Set aside.

2. In large bowl stir together flour, cocoa, baking soda, cinnamon, and salt. In smaller bowl stir together oil, sugar, eggs, yogurt and vanilla. Add to flour mixture along with zucchini, stirring until well blended. Pour into prepared pan; smooth top. Sprinkle chocolate chips and nuts evenly on top.

3. Bake in preheated 350°F oven for 25 to 30 minutes, or until toothpick inserted into centre comes out clean. Cool then cut into squares. Freezes well.

Chocolate Sour Cream Cake

Makes 1 9-inch cake

A quick dessert that everyone will love. Serve it warm with a dollop of vanilla ice cream or frozen yogurt.

1/3 cup soft butter
1 cup granulated sugar (1st amount)
2 eggs
1 1/4 cups all-purpose flour
1/4 cup cocoa
1 1/2 teaspoons baking powder
1 teaspoon baking soda
1 teaspoon cinnamon
1 cup light sour cream
1/3 cup chocolate chips
1 teaspoon sugar to garnish (2nd amount)

1. In large bowl, beat together until smooth, butter and 1 cup sugar. Add eggs one at a time; beat until smooth.

2. In medium bowl, stir together flour, cocoa, baking powder, baking soda and cinnamon. Add to egg mixture; mix well. Add sour cream; stir until well mixed. Spoon batter into greased 9-inch baking pan. Smooth top. Sprinkle with chocolate chips and 1 tablespoon sugar.

3. Bake in preheated 350°F oven for 35 minutes, or until toothpick inserted into centre comes out clean. Freezes well.

Chocolate Fudge Nut Torte (no flour)

10 to 12 servings

Serve this elegant, rich cake as the perfect ending to your next dinner party. Garnish it with the prettiest edible flowers from your garden, set in a wreath of beautiful but simply made Chocolate Leaves *(see next page)*.

Torte:

> 4 ounces good-quality semi-sweet chocolate, preferably Belgian
> 1/2 cup butter
> 2/3 cup sugar
> Zest of 1 orange
> 1 tablespoon Grand Marnier or other orange liqueur
> 3 eggs
> 2 cups finely ground walnuts, almonds, hazelnuts or pecans

Glaze:

> 6 ounces good quality semi-sweet chocolate
> 6 tablespoons butter
> 1 tablespoon light corn syrup

1. Grease and flour an 8-inch springform pan. Line bottom of pan with parchment or waxed paper.

2. **Torte:** Melt 4 ounces chocolate and 1/2 cup butter over low heat. Stir in sugar and zest. Cool 5 minutes. Stir in liqueur. Add eggs one at a time, mixing well after each addition. Stir in nuts.

3. Pour batter into prepared pan. Bake in preheated 375°F oven for 25 minutes or until firm almost to the centre. If too soft and fudge-like in the centre, bake for 5 minutes more, but do not overbake.

4. Cool completely before removing sides of pan. Remove paper from bottom of cake. Place cake on rack set on top of a piece of waxed paper. If making ahead, wrap and freeze unglazed torte. Add glaze to fully defrosted torte on the day you plan to serve it.

5. **Glaze:** Melt chocolate and butter together over low heat. Stir in corn syrup. Pour glaze carefully over cake, letting the glaze flow to coat the top and sides of the cake. Do not spread with a knife. Let the glazed cake cool completely. Transfer cake to serving platter. Decorate top with edible flowers and chocolate leaves.

6. Serve small slices at room temperature, garnished with a sprinkling of edible gold, icing sugar or cocoa.

Chocolate Leaves

1. Use clean, dry leaves that have not been sprayed with chemicals. Rose leaves are easy to work with.

2. Melt 2 to 4 ounces semi-sweet chocolate in top of double boiler. Use a small brush or knife to brush a thick layer of melted chocolate onto the back (non-shiny) side of the leaves, taking care not to let chocolate drip onto the shiny side. Place coated leaves chocolate-side-up on waxed paper-covered tray. Refrigerate until chocolate hardens.

3. Carefully peel leaf away from chocolate. If chocolate leaf breaks, melt and start again. Store chocolate leaves in a covered container in the refrigerator or a cool, dry place. Can be made up to one week ahead.

Edible Flowers

Choose clean flowers that have not been sprayed with chemicals. Avoid commercially grown flowers unless you know they are safe to eat. Choose from: pansies, Johnny Jump-ups, rose petals, wild violets, calendulas, nasturtiums, all herb blossoms, bachelor buttons, carnations, forget-me-nots, impatiens, honeysuckle, lilac, petunias, portulaca, snapdragons, chrysanthemums, chive blossoms, day lilies, dandelions, daisies, hibiscus, scented geraniums, hollyhocks, marigolds, and violas. If you aren't sure if a flower is safe to eat, avoid it.

Ginger Pear Upside-Down Cake

6 to 8 servings

At the beginning of our first discussion about which recipes would be in this book, Leanne said, "Of course the Ginger Pear Upside-Down Cake is in?" It wasn't then, but is now. This one is for you, Lee!

2 tablespoons melted butter
1/4 cup brown sugar
1 large ripe pear, peeled, cored, thinly sliced
1/4 cup slivered candied ginger
1 1/4 cups all-purpose flour
1 teaspoon baking soda
1/2 teaspoon each: ground ginger and cinnamon
1/8 teaspoon each: nutmeg, cloves and salt
1/4 cup shortening or butter
1/2 cup granulated sugar
1/2 cup molasses
1/3 cup boiling water
1 egg

1. Butter an 8-inch round or square baking pan. Add melted butter and brown sugar; stir to mix. Spread evenly in pan. Arrange pear slices on butter mixture. Sprinkle candied ginger over pear slices.

2. In small bowl, stir together flour, baking soda, spices and salt. In large bowl, cream together shortening and granulated sugar. Stir in molasses. Add flour mixture and boiling water alternately to molasses mixture; mix well. Stir in egg.

3. Pour batter into prepared pan, being careful not to move pear slices. Bake in preheated 350°F oven for 25 to 35 minutes, or until toothpick inserted near centre of cake comes out clean. Let stand in pan for 5 minutes, then loosen edges with a knife and carefully invert cake onto serving platter. Serve warm with sweetened whipped cream, vanilla frozen yogurt or ice cream.

Orange Mini Cheesecake

Serves 2

A tasty little treat for one or two—perfect for the cheesecake lover who lives alone.

> 1/4 cup chocolate wafer crumbs
> 1 tablespoon sugar (1st amount)
> 1 tablespoon melted butter
> 1 small package (4 ounces/125 g) light cream cheese, softened
> 1 tablespoon sugar (2nd amount)
> 1 egg
> Grated zest of 1 orange
> 2 teaspoons orange liqueur or orange juice
> 2 tablespoons light sour cream
> 2 teaspoons orange marmalade

1. Combine chocolate wafer crumbs, 1 tablespoon sugar and melted butter in small bowl; stir to mix. Press onto bottom of lightly greased 4-inch baking dish or 3 custard cups. Bake in preheated 300°F oven for 5 minutes.

2. In medium bowl, beat cream cheese, 1 tablespoon sugar, egg, zest and liqueur or juice together until smooth. Pour over baked shell. Bake in preheated 300°F oven for 20 to 25 minutes, or until cheesecake appears set to centre when dish is shaken slightly.

3. In small bowl, stir together sour cream and marmalade. Spread evenly over cheesecake. Return to oven for 5 minutes more. Cool completely, then wrap and refrigerate overnight. Serve garnished with thinly sliced orange.

Rhubarb Orange Upside-Down Cake

Makes 1 9-inch cake

The sweetness of orange in the cake is the perfect complement to the tangy rhubarb topping. Serve at your first barbecue this summer.

2 tablespoons melted butter
3/4 cup brown sugar
2 tablespoons orange juice (1st amount)
4 cups diced fresh rhubarb
2 cups all-purpose flour
1 tablespoon baking powder
1/2 teaspoon salt
1/4 cup sugar
Zest of 1 large orange
1/3 cup cold butter, cut into chunks
1 egg, beaten
2/3 cup milk
1/3 cup orange juice (2nd amount)

1. Melt butter in 9-inch round or square baking pan. Stir in brown sugar and 2 tablespoons orange juice; stir to mix. Spread evenly to cover bottom of pan. Sprinkle rhubarb over this mixture in pan in an even, attractive pattern—cake will be inverted to serve. Set aside.

2. Measure flour, baking powder, salt, sugar and orange zest into medium bowl (if mixing by hand) or food processor. If mixing by hand, cut in cold butter until mixture resembles coarse meal. If using food processor, chop butter into flour using pulse motion, until mixture resembles coarse meal.

3. Mix egg, milk and 1/3 cup orange juice together in small bowl; add to flour mixture. If mixing by hand, stir with fork until just combined. In food processor, pulse until just combined. The batter will be stiff.

4. Spoon batter over rhubarb. Spread to completely cover rhubarb evenly with batter.

5. Bake in preheated 350°F oven for 30 to 40 minutes, or until toothpick inserted into the centre of the cake comes out clean. Cool in pan for 10 minutes.

6. Run a sharp knife around edge of pan to loosen cake. Invert carefully onto rimmed cake plate. Serve warm with sweetened whipped cream or vanilla ice cream.

Sugar-Free Strawberry Rhubarb Sauce

Makes about 1 1/2 cups

Make several batches when rhubarb and strawberries are in season, and freeze in small containers to enjoy later in the year.

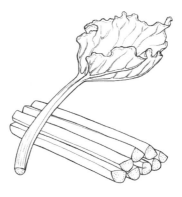

    1 cup sliced strawberries
    1 cup chopped rhubarb
    3 tablespoons apple or orange juice concentrate
    2 teaspoons cornstarch

1. In 4-cup glass measure or microwave-safe bowl (or in medium saucepan on stovetop: add 3 tablespoons water if cooking on stove), combine strawberries and rhubarb. Microwave on High for 3 minutes (or cook on stovetop over medium heat) until rhubarb is tender.

2. Stir in apple or orange juice concentrate and cornstarch. Stir to mix well. Microwave on High 1 minute, or simmer on stovetop until thickened.

3. Chill until cold. Taste; add more fruit juice concentrate if needed to suit your tastes.

4. Serve for breakfast on toast, scones or English muffins, or for dessert on vanilla ice cream. Freezes well.

Grand Marnier Fuitcakes

Makes 12 small fruitcakes

I developed this recipe for *Canadian Living's Holiday Best 2000* magazine. Each of the 12 small fruitcakes weighs about 8 ounces, just the right size for gift giving or to sell at holiday bake sales.

1 1/2 cups golden raisins
1 cup chopped dried apricots
1/2 cup Grand Marnier or other orange liqueur
1 1/4 cups each: red and green glazed cherries
2 cups glazed pineapple chunks
1 1/2 cups mixed peel
1 cup mixed candied fruit or candied citron
1 1/2 cups whole blanched almonds
1 cup pecan halves
3 cups all-purpose flour, divided
1 cup butter, softened
1 cup granulated sugar
4 eggs
2 unpeeled seedless oranges, cut into 8 pieces

1. In large bowl, stir together raisins, apricots and Grand Marnier. Cover bowl with plastic wrap; let stand 1 hour. Stir in cherries, pineapple, mixed peel and candied fruit. Mix well. Cover bowl with plastic wrap; let stand at room temperature overnight.

2. **Next day:** Stir 1 cup of the flour and the almonds and pecans into the fruit mixture. Set aside.

3. Line a 13 x 9-inch baking pan with parchment or waxed paper. Butter well or spray with vegetable oil spray; set aside.

4. In medium bowl, cream butter and sugar until light and fluffy. Beat in eggs one at a time.

5. In food processor, finely chop the oranges. Stir into butter mixture along with remaining flour. Pour over fruit mixture; mix well. Batter will be stiff.

6. Spread batter evenly in pan; smooth top. Set a pan of boiling water on bottom rack of preheated 275°F oven. Bake fruitcake on middle rack for 2 hours, or until cake is lightly browned and firm to the touch. A toothpick inserted into the centre should come out clean and only slightly sticky.

7. Cool cake in pan on cooling rack. Cover and refrigerate overnight before cutting into 12 bars. Cut cake lengthwise in half, then crosswise in half. Cut each quarter into 3 bars, 2 x 4-inches. Wrap well before storing in a cool place for several weeks before serving.

No~Fail Pastry

Mix together in
medium bowl
until smooth:
2/3 cup lard or
shortening
1/3 cup boiling water

Stir in with a fork:
2 cups cake
and pastry flour
3/4 teaspoon salt

Dough is very soft.
Cover and refrigerate
for 30 to 60 minutes
before rolling.
Makes pastry for
one 8-inch,
2-crust pie.

Pecan Pie

I often take one or two of these to potluck suppers. There are never any leftovers!

3 eggs
2/3 cup sugar
Pinch salt
1 cup corn syrup
1/4 cup butter, melted
1 cup pecan halves
1 unbaked 9-inch pastry shell

1. In medium bowl, whisk together eggs, sugar, salt, corn syrup and melted butter.

2. Arrange pecan halves in decorative pattern in pastry shell. Slowly and carefully pour egg mixture over pecans, trying not to move them. They will float to the surface of the filling, but usually end up in the right place after baking.

3. Bake in preheated 350°F oven for 50 minutes, or until pastry is browned and sharp knife inserted into filling near centre comes out clean.

Plum Tarte

Serves 6 to 8

Mix and match the fruits used in this lovely rustic tarte to suit the season: perhaps apples, pears and cranberries in the fall, raspberries and peaches in the summer, strawberries and rhubarb in the spring.

> 1 recipe of your favourite pie pastry,
>   or 1 package puff pastry dough, defrosted
> 1/2 cup finely chopped nuts
> 1/4 cup sugar
> 1/4 cup flour
> 15 to 20 prune plums, washed, halved lengthwise
> Granulated sugar, to garnish
> 1/4 cup fruit jelly melted and mixed with 1 tablespoon brandy
>   or Kirsch

1. Roll pastry on a lightly floured board to 1/8-inch thick. Wrap around rolling pin and unroll onto a lightly greased or parchment-lined large jelly roll pan or pizza pan. If using puff pastry, pierce surface all over with the tines of a fork.

2. Combine nuts, 1/4 cup sugar and flour in a small bowl. Sprinkle evenly over pastry, leaving a 1 1/2-inch border with no nut mixture on it. Arrange plums in a single layer on top of nut mixture. Fold outer edge of pastry over outermost edge of fruit. Pinch dough together to close gaps so that juices will be contained during baking.

3. Sprinkle a bit of sugar lightly over fruit and pastry. Bake in preheated 400°F oven for 45 minutes to 1 hour, or until crust is golden.

4. Heat jelly and brandy together until jelly melts. Brush this glaze over fruit and crust once tarte has cooled slightly.

5. Serve tarte warm or at room temperature with sweetened whipped cream or Crème Fraîche *(see sidebar)*.

Crème Fraîche

1 1/2 cups
whipping cream
1/2 cup sour cream

Stir ingredients together. Let stand at room temperature for 6 hours, or until thickened. Stir; cover and refrigerate until needed.

Bumbleberry Crumble Pie

When the first stalks of rosy rhubarb ripen in your spring garden, make this pie with the last of the frozen berries and any other fruit you have available. Use the fruit combination you like best, just be sure to keep the total volume of fruit at 5 1/2 to 6 cups. Change the sugar quantity to suit the fruit.

Pastry to line 1 deep 9-inch pie plate
(see No-Fail Pastry recipe, page 114)

Filling:
3/4 cup sugar
1 1/2 tablespoons flour
1 1/2 tablespoons cornstarch
1 1/2 cups chopped rhubarb (in 1/2-inch pieces)
1 1/2 cups peeled chopped apple
1 cup raspberries, fresh or defrosted and drained
1 cup blueberries or strawberries, fresh or defrosted and drained
1/2 cup cranberries, fresh or defrosted and drained
1 tablespoon fresh lemon juice

Topping:
1/3 cup brown sugar
1/4 cup flour
3 tablespoons cold butter, chopped
1/4 cup rolled or quick oats
1/4 cup chopped pecans or walnuts

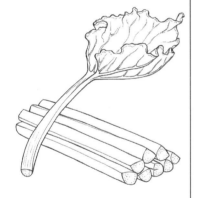

1. Press pastry into a deep 9-inch pie plate. Set aside.

2. **Filling:** In small bowl, combine sugar, flour and cornstarch. Set aside. In large bowl, stir together rhubarb, apples and sugar mixture until well mixed. Add all berries; stir gently just until mixed, being careful not to crush berries. Spoon filling into pie shell. Sprinkle with lemon juice.

3. **Topping:** Mix brown sugar and flour in small bowl or food processor. Add butter. If mixing by hand, use fingertips or pastry cutter to blend butter into flour mixture until mixture resembles coarse crumbs. Use pulse motion of food processor to mix to coarse crumbs. Stir in oats and nuts; mix or pulse just until crumbly. Sprinkle topping evenly over filling.

4. Bake in preheated 425°F oven for 15 minutes. Lower oven temperature to 350°F and bake for 35 to 40 minutes more, or until pastry and topping are nicely browned and filling is bubbly. Serve warm or at room temperature, topped with a scoop of vanilla ice cream.

Frozen Lime Cream Pie

Makes 1 9-inch pie

Lighter than a classic Key Lime Pie, and possibly more welcome at the end of a hearty dinner.

Crust:

1 cup graham wafer crumbs
1/2 cup coconut
2 tablespoons sugar
2 tablespoons butter, melted
2 tablespoons water

Filling:

Zest of 2 limes
1 tablespoon unflavoured gelatin (1 packet)
1/2 cup sugar (1st amount)
1/2 cup lime juice
1/4 cup water
4 eggs, separated
Few drops green food colouring
1/3 cup sugar (2nd amount)
3/4 cup whipping cream, whipped
1 teaspoon crushed lime hard candies, to garnish

1. **Crust:** In small bowl, stir together crumbs, coconut and sugar. Add melted butter and water; stir with a fork until dry ingredients are all moistened. Spoon mixture into a greased 9-inch pie plate. Press mixture firmly into pan, covering bottom, sides and rim. Bake in preheated 350°F oven for 10 minutes. Cool completely.

2. **Filling:** Remove zest from 2 limes; set zest aside.

3. In medium saucepan, whisk together gelatin, 1/2 cup sugar, lime juice, water and egg yolks. Turn heat to medium; cook and stir with whisk until mixture thickens and boils.

4. Remove from heat. Add green food colouring to desired colour (not too dark!). Transfer mixture to large stainless steel bowl. Refrigerate 30 to 60 minutes, checking often, until the mixture has the consistency of thick, raw egg white. Stir in lime zest. While mixture chills, whip cream and egg whites until foamy; continue beating, gradually adding 1/3 cup sugar, to form stiff peaks.

5. As soon as refrigerated gelatin mixture reaches desired consistency, carefully fold in whipped cream and beaten egg whites, until mixture is a uniform colour with no white streaks.

6. Spoon into cooled graham wafer shell. Smooth top. Sprinkle crushed candy over top to garnish. Wrap and refrigerate for 4 hours or freeze until firm. Pie can be served either chilled (refrigerated) or frozen. Can be prepared and frozen up to 3 weeks ahead.

Walnut Meringue Ice Cream Pie

Serves 6 to 8

Fill this luscious, chewy crust with your favourite ice cream and put it in the freezer, ready to serve to family and friends at a moment's notice.

Walnut Meringue Shell:
    2 egg whites
    Pinch salt and cream of tartar
    1/2 cup sugar
    2 cups finely chopped walnuts

Filling:
    1 to 2 litres of your favourite flavour of ice cream

Toppings:
    Warm chocolate sauce, homemade or purchased
    Sliced sweetened fresh berries, peaches, mango, or other soft fruit

1. **Walnut Meringue Shell**: Butter or spray a 9-inch pie plate well. Set aside.

2. In medium mixing bowl, beat egg white with salt and cream of tartar to soft peaks. Beat in sugar a bit at a time. Continue beating until stiff peaks form. Gently fold in walnuts.

3. Spoon walnut mixture into prepared pan, spreading evenly with a wet spatula to cover bottom, sides and rim of pan. Bake in preheated 400°F oven for 10 minutes. Use fork to pierce and deflate centre to form a shell. Reduce oven temperature to 350°F. Bake for 15 minutes, or until crust is light brown and firm. Cool completely. Wrap and refrigerate until cold.

4. Fill cold shell with scoops of ice cream. Smooth top. Wrap and freeze at this point if desired.

5. **To serve:** Cut into wedges and add topping of choice.

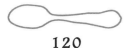

Biscuit Tortoni in Chocolate Cups

Serves 2

This made-for-two confection can easily be doubled or tripled for entertaining. If desired, use purchased chocolate cups, or spoon filling directly into muffin papers, omitting the chocolate cups altogether.

Chocolate cups:

    2 ounces semi-sweet Belgian chocolate, melted over low heat or in microwave using low power (about 1/3 cup chocolate chips or chopped chocolate)

Filling:

    2 tablespoons crushed toasted almonds
    2 tablespoons crumbled macaroons or amaretti cookies
    1 tablespoon whipping cream (1st amount)
    1/3 cup whipping cream (2nd amount)
    2 teaspoons icing sugar
    1 1/2 teaspoons dark rum
    1 maraschino or candied cherry, cut in half, to garnish

1. **Chocolate cups:** Spoon half of the chocolate into each of 2 muffin papers; spread chocolate to completely cover bottom and sides. Place filled papers in a muffin pan; refrigerate until firm. Peel off paper; refrigerate until needed. Can be made ahead and stored in a cool place in an airtight container.

2. **Filling:** In small bowl, stir together almonds, crumbled cookies and 1 tablespoon whipping cream; let stand for 10 minutes.

3. Whip 1/3 cup of cream until foamy; add sugar and rum; beat until stiff. Fold in almond mixture.

4. Spoon filling into chocolate cups; freeze until firm. Can prepare up to 1 week ahead. Store in freezer in an airtight container.

5. To serve, top each biscuit tortoni with half of a cherry and a sprinkling of either chopped toasted almonds, grated chocolate or edible gold.

Belgian Chocolate Fondue

Serves 8

This classic dessert was at its peak of popularity when Read and I were married in 1969, which explains why we received five fondue pots for wedding gifts! It's not surprising that such a delicious treat is topping the dessert charts again today.

> 10 ounces Belgian bittersweet chocolate, chopped
> 1/2 to 3/4 cup light cream
> 3 tablespoons brandy, rum or fruit liqueur of choice *(optional)*

To dip:

> orange or clementine segments, banana and mango chunks, strawberries, kiwi wedges, dried apricots, canned pineapple spears, walnut or pecan halves, mini cream puffs filled with vanilla ice cream *(recipe on next page)*

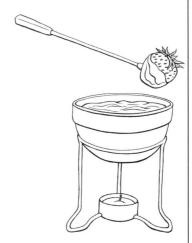

1. Over very low heat or in top of double boiler over hot but not boiling water, melt chocolate and cream together, stirring until chocolate melts. Remove from heat; stir in flavouring.

2. Transfer mixture to fondue pot set over warming candle. Offer a variety of dipping foods to guests.

Mini Cream Puffs

Makes about 5 dozen puffs

3/4 cup water
6 tablespoons butter
3/4 cup flour
3 eggs
Dash of salt

1. Combine water and butter in medium saucepan; heat to boiling.

2. Remove from heat. Add flour and salt all at once. Stir until mixture pulls away from sides of pan and forms a ball. Cook and stir 1 minute over medium heat. Remove from heat.

3. Add eggs one at a time, beating well after each addition. Add enough egg to make fairly stiff dough. You may not need the whole final egg.

4. Drop dough by scant spoonfuls or pipe small mounds onto a lightly greased or parchment-lined baking sheet. Bake in preheated 425°F oven for about 15 minutes, or until puffed and lightly browned.

5. At serving time, let each guest fill cooled puffs with vanilla ice cream to dip into fondue. To make ahead, puffs can be filled with ice cream and frozen until serving time, ready to dip in chocolate fondue or drizzle with warm chocolate sauce for a quick dessert.

Fruit Cobbler

Serves 6 to 8

An old-fashioned favourite that's as warming and welcome today as it was years ago.

Biscuit Topping:

1 cup all-purpose flour
1 tablespoon baking powder
1 tablespoon sugar
Pinch of salt
1/4 cup shortening or butter
1/4 cup light sour cream
1 egg
Granulated sugar to garnish

Fruit Mixture:

6 cups prepared soft fruit: a combination of peeled sliced peaches, fresh blueberries, strawberries or raspberries, sliced nectarines or apricots, etc.
1 tablespoon lemon or orange juice
2/3 to 3/4 cup sugar mixed with 2 tablespoons cornstarch

1. **Biscuit Topping:** In medium bowl, mix together flour, baking powder, sugar and salt. Cut in shortening or butter with pastry cutter until crumbly.

2. In small bowl, mix together sour cream and egg. Add to flour mixture; stir until dough is smooth and soft. Turn out onto a lightly floured board. Knead 8 times.

3. Roll into a 9-inch round or square, depending on baking pan shape. Cut into wedges or squares. Set aside.

4. **Fruit Mixture:** Mix fruit and lemon or orange juice together in 9-inch square or round baking pan or 2.5 litre casserole. Sprinkle sugar and cornstarch mixture (adjust sugar quantity to suit sweetness of fruit being used) over fruit; toss gently to mix. Cover pan with foil. Bake in preheated 400°F oven for 10 minutes. Remove foil.

5. Arrange biscuit pieces on top of heated fruit. Sprinkle with sugar to garnish. Bake in preheated 400°F oven for 25 to 30 minutes, or until biscuit topping is golden brown and fruit is tender and bubbly.

6. Serve warm with Crème Fraîche *(see page 115)*, sweetened whipped cream, or vanilla ice cream or yogurt.

Variation

Substitute 2 cups of any other frozen fruit that you have on hand: strawberries, blueberries, sliced peaches or a combination of your favourites.

John's Quick Raspberry Ice Cream

Thanks to John Whiting for sharing the recipe for this creamy and delicious ice cream treat.

> 2 cups unsweetened frozen raspberries—*not* defrosted
> 1 cup chilled whipping cream
> 1/3 cup sugar

1. Place frozen berries in food processor work bowl. Add whipping cream and sugar. Pulse several times to coarsely chop, then process for 1 minute, or until mixture is smooth and thick. Ice cream is ready as soon as it is creamy.

2. Serve immediately, or transfer to bowl and place in freezer until serving time.

Tropical Fruit Filo Sundaes

Serves 6

Make and bake the filo cups a few days ahead, then put this lovely dessert together in minutes. Your guests will be dazzled!

Filo cups:
> 2 sheets of filo pastry
> 1 1/2 tablespoons melted butter

Filling and garnishes:
> Mango sherbet or your choice of ice cream
> Prepared fruit of choice: sliced strawberries, kiwi, mango and
> bananas, green or red grapes, orange segments, pineapple, etc.,
> gently mixed and sweetened to taste with sugar and fruit liqueur
> Icing sugar, melted chocolate to drizzle, and mint leaves

1. **To make filo cups:** Place 1 sheet of filo on work surface. Using scissors, pizza wheel or sharp knife, cut filo into three 5-inch-wide strips. Brush each strip lightly with butter. Fold into thirds. Carefully press into muffin cups. Repeat with remaining filo. Bake in preheated 350°F oven for 5 to 7 minutes, or until shells are brown and crisp. Remove from muffin pan and set aside.

2. **To assemble:** Place filo cups on individual dessert plates. Place a scoop of sherbet or ice cream in each cup. Spoon fruit over. Drizzle chocolate over, if using. Dust with icing sugar shaken through a small sieve. Garnish plate with mint leaves. Serve at once.

Remember, when a dish doesn't turn out exactly as planned, you haven't failed, you've invented a new recipe!

The Last Word—More Help for Busy Cooks

Casserole Substitutes

When you don't have the exact pan called for in a recipe, purchase inexpensive foil baking pans or substitute the following:

4-cup or 1 litre casserole: a 9-inch pie plate or an 8-inch round cake pan

6-cup or 1.5 litre: 9-inch cake pan or a 10-inch pie plate.

8-cup or 2 litre: 8-inch square baking pan, an 11 x 7-inch baking pan or a 9 x 5 x 3 loaf pan

10 cup or 2.5 litre: 9-inch square baking pan or 12 x 8-inch baking pan

12 cup or 3 litre: a 13 x 9 baking pan

Larger quantities: use a roasting pan for large quantities.

Emergency Substitutions

Sour milk or buttermilk: 1 cup = 1 tbsp vinegar or lemon juice and enough milk to make 1 cup

Sour cream: 1 cup = 1 cup plain yogurt

Unsweetened chocolate: 1-ounce square = 3 tbsp cocoa and 1 tbsp melted butter or margarine

Herbs: 1 tbsp fresh = 1 tsp dried

Lemon juice: 1 tsp = 1/2 tsp plain white vinegar

Tomato sauce: 1 cup = 1/2 cup tomato paste and 1/2 cup water

Breadcrumbs: 1 cup fresh = 2 slices of bread

1 cup dried = 3 slices of toast

or 3/4 cup cracker or cornflake crumbs

Index

A

All-Seasons Pesto Sauce 85
All-Day Beef Stew 38
Antipasto, Make-Ahead 16
Appetizers
    Antipasto, Make-Ahead 16
    Baked Sesame Tortilla Wedges 15
    Cheddar Puffs 12
    Crab Melts 11
    Guacamole, Great 13
    Italian Stuffed Mushrooms 14
    "Lighter than Hummus" Chickpea Spread 15
    Maple Chicken Wings 17
    Marinated Mushrooms 18
    Minted Melon Limeade 13
    Roasted Red Pepper Hummus 19
    Seafood Appetizer Platter 20
    Smoked Salmon Cheesecake 22
    Sun-Dried Tomato Tapenade 21
    Warm Herb and Spice Olives 24
Apple Pecan Strata 30
Asparagus
    Asparagus Cheese Soufflé 66
    Chicken Asparagus Packets 47
    Grilled, with Tarragon Vinaigrette 82
    Spring Vegetable Omelette 68
    Toppings for 82
Avocado
    Great Guacamole 13
    Shrimp and Avocado Salad 76

B

Baked Sesame Tortilla Wedges 15
Balsamic Dill Vinaigrette 84
Beef: See *Main Dishes*
Beef Saté with Peanut Sauce 40
Beef Stew, All-Day 38
Belgian Chocolate Fondue 122

Berry Delicious Fruit Shake 31
Beverages: See *Appetizers, Brunch, Kids Cook*
Biscuit Tortoni in Chocolate Cups 121
Black Bean and Sausage Soup 92
Bread Bowl 78
Breads: See *Appetizers, Brunch, Kids Cook*
Broccoli and Carrot Stir-Fry 83
Brownies, Zucchini Chocolate 104
Brunch
    Apple Pecan Strata 30
    Fruit-Full Orange Bran Muffins 26
    Mexican Coffee 30
    Pumpkin Muffins 27
    Rhubarb Toast Topper 25
    Strawberry Rhubarb Muffins 28
    Sugar-Free Strawberry Rhubarb Sauce 111
    Sunshine Fruit Bowl 25
    Vegetable Confetti Mini Muffins 29
Bulgur, Tabouleh with a Twist 79
Bumbleberry Crumble Pie 116
Butter Tart Squares 103

C

Cabbage: Red Cabbage Salad 74
Cakes: See *Sweets*
Carrot and Broccoli Stir-Fry 83
Carrot and Zucchini Sauté 84
Carrots: See *Salads, Side Dishes, Soups*
Cassoulet, Slow Cooker 53
Cheddar Herb Dumplings 39
Cheddar Puffs 12
Cheese
    Asparagus Cheese Soufflé 66
    Cheddar Herb Dumplings 39
    Cheddar Puffs 12
    Green Salad with Pears, Chèvre
       and Sugared Pecans 72
    Hazelnut-Crusted Chèvre 77
    Mexican Macaroni and Cheese 64

Parmesan Cream Garnish for Soup 95
Shredded quantities 23
Swiss Raclette for Four 65
Vegetable and Cheese Frittata 69
Vegetable and Cheese Torta 70
Cheesecake
    Orange Mini 109
    Smoked Salmon 22
Chicken, See *Poultry*
Chicken Asparagus Packets 47
Chocolate: See *Sweets*
Chickpea Spread, "Lighter than Hummus" 15
Chocolate Fudge Nut Torte (no flour) 106
Chocolate Leaves 107
Chocolate Sour Cream Cake 105
Chunky Oatmeal Cookies with
    Dates and Walnuts 100
Cider-Glazed Pork Tenderloin
    with Caramelized Onion and Apple Stuffing 44
Cobbler, Fruit 124
Coffee, Mexican 30
Cook For One—You're Worth It!
    Biscuit Tortoni in Chocolate Cups 121
    Coquilles St. Jacques 56
    Egg and Veggie Wrap 67
    Ginger Lime Salmon in Parchment 60
    Greek-Style Grilled Chicken 50
    Grilled Vegetable Packets 89
    One-Rib Prime Rib Roast 42
    Orange Mini Cheesecake 109
    Pesto Broiled Tomatoes 85
    Quick Bites 34
    Shrimp and Avocado Salad 76
    Spring Vegetable Omelet for One 68
    Vegetable and Cheese Frittata 69
Cookies and Squares: See *Sweets*
Coq au Vin Blanc 48
Coquilles St. Jacques 56
Crab Melts 11
Cranberry Vinegar 77

Cream of Mushroom and Leek Soup 91
Cream Puffs, Mini 123
Crème Fraîche 115
Crunchy Chicken Fingers 36
Cupcake Cones 37
Curried Shrimp with Vegetables, Southeast Asian . . 58

D

Dates: Oatmeal Cookies with
    Dates and Walnuts 100
Desserts: See *Sweets*
Dill-Lemon Mayonnaise 90
Dumplings, Cheddar Herb 39

E

Easy Hollandaise-Type Sauce 82
Eggs
    Apple Pecan Strata 30
    Asparagus Cheese Soufflé 66
    Egg and Veggie Wrap 67
    Quick Egg Fajita 67
    Quick "Egg Roll" 34
    Spring Vegetable Omelette 68
    Tortilla Rolls 34
    Vegetable and Cheese Frittata 69
    Vegetable and Cheese Torta 70

F

Family Sub 35
Fiddlehead and Asparagus Toppings 82
Filo cups 127
Flowers, edible 107
Fondue, Belgian Chocolate 122
Frozen Lime Cream Pie 118
Fruit Cobbler 124
Fruit: See *Brunch, Sweets*
Fruitcakes, Grand Marnier 112
Fruit-Full Orange Bran Muffins 26
Fudge, No-Fail Chocolate 99

G

Garlic
  Roasting 96
  Roasted Carrot, Onion and Garlic Soup 95
  Roasted Garlic Vichyssoise 96
Gazpacho 93
Ginger Lime Salmon In Parchment 60
Ginger Pear Upside-Down Cake 108
Glaze, Maple Orange for Ham 46
Grand Marnier Fruitcakes 112
Great Guacamole 13
Greek-Style Grilled Chicken 50
Green Salad with Pears,
  Chèvre and Sugared Pecans 72
Grilled Asparagus with Tarragon Vinaigrette 82
Grilled Herbed Lamb Chops 43
Grilled Potato Halves 86
Grilled Tilapia 62
Grilled Vegetable Packets 89
Guacamole, Great 13

H

Ham, Maple Orange Glaze for 46
Hazelnut Apricot Rice Ring 81
Herbes de Provence 54
Hot Cross Buns, Bunnies 32
Hummus: See *Appetizers*

I

Ice Cream
  John's Quick Raspberry Ice Cream 126
  Walnut Meringue Ice Cream Pie 120
Italian Mussel Soup 94
Italian Stuffed Mushrooms 14

J

John's Quick Raspberry Ice Cream 126

K

Kebobs: See *Main Dishes*
Kids Cook
  Berry Delicious Fruit Shake 31
  Crunchy Chicken Fingers 36
  Cupcake Cones 37
  Family Sub 35
  Hot Cross Bunnies, Buns 32
  Pancake Initials 33
  Pizza Rolls 34
  Tortilla Rolls 34
  Quick "Egg Roll" 34
  Vegetable Wraps or Pockets 34

L

Lamb: Grilled Herbed Lamb Chops 43
Lasagna, Mexican 55
Leeks, Cream of Mushroom and Leek Soup 91
Lemon Squares 102
Lemon Grass, about 41
"Lighter than Hummus" Chickpea Spread 15
Lime, Frozen Lime Cream Pie 118
Limeade, Minted Melon Limeade 13

M

Macaroni and Cheese, Mexican 64
Main Dishes
  All-Day Beef Stew 38
  Asparagus Cheese Soufflé 66
  Beef Saté with Peanut Sauce 40
  Cheddar Herb Dumplings 39
  Chicken Asparagus Packets 47
  Cider-Glazed Pork Tenderloin with
    Caramelized Onion and Apple Stuffing 44
  Coq au Vin Blanc 48
  Coquilles St. Jacques 56
  Egg and Veggie Wrap 67
  Ginger Lime Salmon In Parchment 60
  Greek-Style Grilled Chicken 50
  Grilled Herbed Lamb Chops 43
  Grilled Tilapia 62
  Maple Mustard Pork Tenderloin 46
  Maple Orange Glaze for Ham 46
  Mexican Lasagna 55
  Mexican Macaroni and Cheese 64
  One-Rib Prime Rib Roast 42
  Provençal Turkey Breast 54

Quick Egg Fajita 67
Quick Mexican Chicken 52
Seafood Grilled on a Cedar Plank 63
Shrimp, Chicken and Pineapple Kebobs 57
Slow Cooker Cassoulet 53
Southeast Asian Curried
     Shrimp with Vegetables 58
Spring Vegetable Omelette 68
Summer Salad with Grilled
     Chicken and Strawberries 51
Swiss Raclette for Four 65
Vegetable and Cheese Frittata 69
Vegetable and Cheese Torta 70
Make-Ahead Antipasto 16
Make-Ahead Mashed Potato Casserole 88
Maple Chicken Wings 17
Maple Mustard Pork Tenderloin 46
Maple Orange Glaze for Ham 46
Marinated Carrot Salad with Fresh Dill 73
Marinated Mushrooms 18
Mayonnaise, Dill-Lemon 90
Meringue, Walnut Meringue Ice Cream Pie 120
Mexican Chicken, Quick 52
Mexican Coffee 30
Mexican Lasagna 55
Mexican Macaroni and Cheese 64
Mini Cream Puffs 123
Minted Melon Limeade 13
Muffins: See *Brunch*
Mushrooms
     Cleaning 14
     Cream of Mushroom and Leek Soup 91
     Italian Stuffed 14
     Marinated 18
Mussels, Italian Mussel Soup 94
Mustard Cream Sauce 82

N
No-Fail Chocolate Fudge 99
No-Fail Pastry 114

O
Oatmeal Cookies with Dates and Walnuts 100
Olives, Warm Herb and Spice 24
One-Rib Prime Rib Roast 42
Onions, chopped quantities 45
Orange Mini Cheesecake 109

P
Pancake Initials 33
Parmesan Cream Garnish for Soup 95
Pastry, No-Fail 114
Peanut Sauce 41
Pecan Pie 114
Peppers, Roasted Red Pepper Hummus 19
Pesto Broiled Tomatoes 85
Pesto Sauce, All-Seasons 85
Pies: See *Sweets*
Pizza Rolls 34
Plum Tarte 115
Pork: See *Main Dishes*
     How to butterfly 44
Poultry: See *Appetizers, Kids Cook, Main Dishes, Salads*
Potatoes: See *Soup, Side Dishes*
     Microwave baked 86
Provençal Turkey Breast 54
Pumpkin Muffins 27

Q
Quick Egg Fajita 67
Quick "Egg Roll" 34
Quick Mexican Chicken 52

R
Raclette, Swiss, for Four 65
Raisin Spice Cookies 101
Raspberry Ice Cream, John's Quick 126
Raspberry Vinegar 72

Red Cabbage Salad 74
Rhubarb Orange Upside-Down Cake 110
Rhubarb
    Strawberry Rhubarb Muffins 28
    Sugar-Free Strawberry Rhubarb Sauce 111
    Rhubarb Toast Topper 25
Rice: See *Side Dishes, Soups*
Risotto with Spring Vegetables 80
Roasted Carrot, Onion and Garlic Soup 95
Roasted Garlic Vichyssoise 96
Roasted Red Peppers, Freezing 19
Roasted Red Pepper Hummus 19

S

Salads
    Bread Bowl 78
    Green Salad with Pears, Chèvre
       and Sugared Pecans 72
    Marinated Carrot Salad with Fresh Dill 73
    Red Cabbage Salad 74
    Salade Niçoise 75
    Shrimp and Avocado Salad 76
    Spinach Salad with Hazelnut Crusted
       Chèvre and Clementine Garnish 77
    Summer Salad with Grilled Chicken
       and Strawberries 51
    Tabouleh with a Twist 79
Salmon: See *Appetizers, Main Dishes*
Salsa, Tropical Fruit 57
Sandwiches: See *Main Dishes, Kids Cook*
Sausage
    Black Bean and Sausage Soup 92
    Slow Cooker Cassoulet 53
Seafood: See *Appetizers, Main Dishes*
    How to choose and store fresh fish 61
Seafood Appetizer Platter 20
Seafood Grilled on a Cedar Plank 63
Shrimp: See *Appetizers, Salads and Main Dishes*
Shrimp and Avocado Salad 76
Shrimp, Chicken and Pineapple Kebobs 57
Side and Vegetable Dishes
    All-Seasons Pesto Sauce 85

Balsamic Dill Vinaigrette 84
Carrot and Broccoli Stir-Fry 83
Carrot and Zucchini Sauté 84
Fiddlehead and Asparagus Toppings 82
Grilled Asparagus with Tarragon Vinaigrette 82
Grilled Potato Halves 86
Grilled Vegetable Packets 89
Hazelnut Apricot Rice Ring 81
Make-Ahead Mashed Potato Casserole 88
Pesto Broiled Tomatoes 85
Risotto with Spring Vegetables 80
Two-Potato Purée 87
Vegetable Medley with
    Dill-Lemon Mayonnaise 90
Slow Cooker Cassoulet 53
Smoked Salmon Cheesecake 22
Soufflé, Asparagus Cheese 66
Soups
    Black Bean and Sausage Soup 92
    Cream of Mushroom and Leek Soup 91
    Gazpacho 93
    Italian Mussel Soup 94
    Parmesan Cream Garnish for Soup 95
    Roasted Carrot, Onion and Garlic Soup 95
    Roasted Garlic Vichyssoise 96
    Tortilla Soup 97
    Wild Rice Soup 98
Sour Cream Cake, Chocolate 105
Southeast Asian Curried Shrimp with Vegetables . . . 58
Spinach Salad with Hazelnut
    Crusted Chèvre and Clementine Garnish 77
Spring Vegetable Omelette 68
Squares: See *Sweets*
Strata, Apple Pecan 30
Strawberries
    Strawberry Rhubarb Muffins 28
    Berry Delicious Fruit Shake 31
    Sugar-Free Strawberry Rhubarb Sauce 111
    Summer Salad with Grilled Chicken
       and Strawberries 51
Sub, Family 35
Sugar-Free Strawberry Rhubarb Sauce 111

Summer Salad with Grilled Chicken
and Strawberries 51
Sun-Dried Tomato Tapenade 21
Sunshine Fruit Bowl 25
Sweet Potatoes: Two-Potato Purée 87
Sweets
   Belgian Chocolate Fondue 122
   Biscuit Tortoni in Chocolate Cups 121
   Bumbleberry Crumble Pie 116
   Butter Tart Squares 103
   Chocolate Fudge Nut Torte (no flour) 106
   Chocolate Leaves 107
   Chocolate Sour Cream Cake 105
   Chunky Oatmeal Cookies
      with Dates and Walnuts 100
   Crème Fraîche 115
   Frozen Lime Cream Pie 118
   Fruit Cobbler 124
   Ginger Pear Upside-Down Cake 108
   Grand Marnier Fruitcakes 112
   John's Quick Raspberry Ice Cream 126
   Lemon Squares 102
   Mini Cream Puffs 123
   No-Fail Chocolate Fudge 99
   No-Fail Pastry 114
   Orange Mini Cheesecake 109
   Pecan Pie 114
   Plum Tarte 115
   Raisin Spice Cookies 101
   Rhubarb Orange Upside-Down Cake 110
   Tropical Fruit Filo Sundaes 127
   Walnut Meringue Ice Cream Pie 120
   Zucchini Chocolate Brownies 104
Swiss Raclette for Four 65

T

Tabouleh with a Twist 79
Tapenade, Sun-Dried Tomato 21
Tilapia, Grilled 62
Tomatoes, Pesto Broiled Tomatoes 85
Torte, Chocolate Fudge Nut 106

Tortillas
   Egg and Veggie Wrap 67
   Mexican Lasagna 55
   Pizza Rolls 34
   Quick Egg Fajita 67
   Quick "Egg Roll" 34
   Tortilla Rolls 34
   Tortilla Soup 97
   Tortilla Wedges, Baked Sesame 15
   Vegetable Wraps or Pockets 34
Tropical Fruit Filo Sundaes 127
Tropical Fruit Salsa 57
Turkey, See *Poultry*
Two-Potato Purée 87

V

Vegetables: See *Side and Vegetable Dishes*
Vegetable and Cheese Frittata 69
Vegetable and Cheese Torta 70
Vegetable Confetti Mini Muffins 29
Vegetable Medley with Dill-Lemon Mayonnaise . . . 90
Vegetable Packets, Grilled 89
Vegetable Wraps or Pockets 34
Vichyssoise, Roasted Garlic 96
Vinegar
   Cranberry 77
   Raspberry 72

W

Walnut Meringue Ice Cream Pie 120
Walnuts: Oatmeal Cookies
   with Dates and Walnuts 100
Warm Herb and Spice Olives 24
Wild Rice Soup 98
Wraps: See *Main Dishes, Kids Cook*

Z

Zucchini
   Carrot and Zucchini Sauté 84
   Zucchini Chocolate Brownies 104

My Favourite Recipes in *PamCooks 2*

We hope you enjoyed cooking with *PamCooks 2: More Favourites from the Trillium Cooking School.*

Also by Pam Collacott:

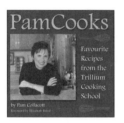

PamCooks, the popular forerunner to *PamCooks 2*, is a delightful collection of easy, quick and delicious recipes.

The Best Of New Wave Cooking, a collection of family-friendly recipes for the microwave oven.

To order any of these cookbooks:

Please send a cheque or money order, payable to Trillium Cooking School, to:

Trillium Cooking School
R.R.#2 North Gower, ON K0A 2T0

PamCooks 2	$18.95
PamCooks	$17.95
The Best Of New Wave Cooking	$10.00

Add $4.00 (postage and handling) for the first book you order + $1.00 for each additional book + 7% GST on your total order.

Be sure to indicate if you would like your books signed and personalized!

Please visit our website:
www.pamcooks.com

The Trillium Cooking School

Not your typical cooking school! Classes are held in a fully modern kitchen in Pam and Read Collacott's 160-year-old renovated log home in a picturesque setting near North Gower, Ontario, a short drive south of Ottawa.

Since 1983, Pam Collacott and a changing list of visiting chefs, cookbook authors and cooking teachers have taught hands-on and demonstration cooking classes on a wide range of topics. Classes such as the popular Friday evening "Dinner at Eight" dinner party classes are booked months, even years, in advance!